MW00613140

DIRECTING
IMPROV

by Asaf Ronen

show the way by getting out of the way

Edited by Jill Bernard

Foreword by Jonathan Pitts

Directing Improv
Show the Way by Getting Out of the Way

By Asaf Ronen

ISBN: 0-9770339-0-2

Published by:
YESand Publishing
98-09 65th Road, Suite 1C
New York, NY 11374

All rights reserved. No part of this book may be reproduced or transmitted in any form or by any means, electronic or mechanical, including photocopying, recording or by any information storage and retrieval system without written permission from the author, except for the inclusion of brief quotations in a review.

Copyright © 2005 Asaf Ronen
Printed in the United States of America

Editor: Jill Bernard
Cover design, illustration: Rob Morse

Library of Congress Control Number: 2005909504
Ronen,Asaf
Directing Improv: Show the Way by Getting Out of the Way / by
Asaf Ronen

This goes out to everyone who

has let me play with them,

to Jill

whose guidance has been invaluable,

and, most of all,

to Adrianne

who has been

the fire in my heart

and under my butt.

TABLE OF CONTENTS

FOREWORD

Improvisational theatre has produced some major talents as well as many working theatre artists, but it is fair to say that most of these artists are actors or writers and not directors. While improv's collective history has produced some great directors (Paul Sills, Mike Nichols, Harold Ramis, Paul Mazursky, Mick Napier, Robert LaPage), there are nowhere near as many directors in improv as there are performers and writers. In fact, often times, directing and directors are often misunderstood as an art, function and role within improv's ensembles, shows and structures. Well here is the first book that may change all that.

Asaf Ronen, a longtime improv artist, has created an excellent book on improv directing and coaching. This book is geared toward beginners through intermediate levels of experienced directors. I'd also recommend it for experienced improvisers who are attempting to direct or coach either a show or an ensemble for the first time. Asaf has clearly defined many problems and situations unique to directing and coaching improv. His chapters of information as well as his conversational tone of writing will immediately make the reader relax and drink in the information Asaf has to share. I also really like his use of other improv directors' stories and observations as a teaching tool for the beginning improv director or coach.

Too often directors are in an isolated role in relationship to the ensemble, directors and coaches don't often have a chance to talk and learn from each other; Asaf's new book on improv directing will also begin to change that too. By focusing on directing and coaching, Asaf's wonderful new book fills a void in the improv canon of published books. If you, as most performers say at some point in their career, "really want to direct," then Asaf's outstanding new book will get you started on the right path!

Jonathan Pitts
Executive Director
Chicago Improv Festival

ABOUT THIS BOOK

There is little accessible training that deals specifically with how to direct improv. In the teaching I have done on the subject, I have found that too many people learn the art of directing and improv simultaneously. This adds several levels of difficulty to a task already fraught with anxiety.

The job of directing is usually thrust upon a person. Perhaps that person has had the benefit of training with experienced professionals in one of the more saturated markets where improvisation is thriving most, or perhaps, has trained in the traditional theatre arts, or has had to educate himself in the art of improv through books, internet sites, and short-lived TV shows. Then, filled with inspiration and enthusiasm, he creates and leads a group or steps into the pilot's seat of whatever rudderless affiliation he is a part.

In this book, I create a vocabulary for improvisational direction to help fledgling directors and teachers better aid their troupes, their students and themselves. This is not a book on how to improvise, but is a companion to the many texts already out there. Rather than learn how to construct a scene, you will learn how to guide others through the construction of a scene.

The vocabulary will be especially important to those in the somewhat maddening position of being the director of a troupe with which they also perform. This dynamic can create further difficulties due to the lessened divide between the personal and the professional mind. As a result, you find situations such as other members freely giving notes or freely dismissing notes based on their director's own performance.

At the time of writing, most of my directing and teaching deals with longform improvisation. There are some passages that specifically address the needs of directing shortform but the majority of the text focuses on scenework. The principles outlined in the book, however, are easily applied to the direction of most games even when not outwardly stated. My techniques are not confined to any one philosophy of improv and I try to show examples from different schools where possible. To further this inclusion, I conducted as many interviews as I could with professional improv teachers and directors.

I wanted the ideas presented to be as accessible as possible, to be firm starting points for the work you need to do, while at the same time malleable enough for you to mold to your voice as you find it.

You will find that there are a lot of extreme scenarios in this book and techniques that are based on worst-case situations. Don't let that scare you into thinking that there is a hellish future awaiting you as a director. I am just making sure that you are prepared for the worst while hoping for the best.

Those without notions of directing will find that the vocabulary will help them in being better directed. They will be able to set their own path of growth without sidelining their director's efforts and be able to raise issues important to them without seeming rebellious.

In the end, I hope that you will find this book empowering, that it helps get your ideas across, fuels new ideas and creatively empowers those around you.

CHAPTER 1: THE JOB OF THE IMPROV DIRECTOR

> The biggest pitfall in my opinion is the belief that the skill set for being an improviser or an actor is enough to manage being a director. It's a whole different thing. I wish every would-be director would be an assistant director, or at least watch and study other directors, before they decided to take it on.
>
> —*Mick Napier*

When directing a scripted play, you start with the product in hand. Granted, it is an incomplete product until interpreted through the eyes of the actors and director, but a set framework nonetheless. This framework is further refined through the rehearsal process until the resulting performance on any given night is as close to the sought vision of the piece with the slightest margin of error possible.

Improvisation, in displaying the process as part of the end product, widens this margin of error. (Of course, in improv there aren't any errors really, since everything is correct. Still, you get the idea.) In directing an ensemble, whether in an ongoing troupe or for a specific performance, our main goal is to minimize this margin, while at the same time realizing that we can never fully eliminate it.

Why would we want to? The risk factor is the reason why most actors improvise; it is the high that we continually chase. The audience also wants to see that risk factor, with the same sensation they get when they see a trapeze artist or a daredevil perform. Besides, have we directors become so pretentious that we think we can control human behavior? Improvisers are creativity junkies who are capable of anything while in the throes of a good scene. Like junkies, they can't be held fully accountable. At the same time, we need them to learn from their "mistakes" so as to not repeat them.

Improv directors, though they were previously performers, sometimes grow to loathe that risk. Every show becomes a huge gamble. They start to categorize their players as "those who get it" and "those who don't get it" or "the players you can count on" versus "the players who have become a burden."

In the coming chapters we are going to move away from those designations and create a new vocabulary.

TYPES OF GROUP DYNAMIC

There are many different structures for an improv group that have been employed to fit different artistic needs. What follows is a strong cross-section of dynamics I have experienced or have seen used, along with some of their strengths and weaknesses. There are probably other structures, but they are most likely variations of those listed below.

While the experience differs from group to group, there are a number of givens that occur based on how the group is structured. In looking at these designations, I factored in four aspects: Vision, Artistic Growth, Personal Dynamic, and Sustainability. Vision describes whether a group has a distinct voice. Artistic Growth deals with the ability to develop the skills of the members as individuals as well as a cohesive unit. Personal Dynamic covers the interactive environment outside the improv scenes, the tensions and the stresses. Sustainability is the level at which the group can be maintained, whether the structure works better for short-term or longer-term projects. There will be exceptions to all the rules but this section will still give you some thoughts on what to look for in any situation in which you may find yourself.

1. Group consensus with no director.

> Have a like-mindedness and be very clear on what it is you're trying to accomplish, what's your goal. It doesn't mean you have to be pigeonholed but get everyone on the same page. Adding to that also being prepared for that to evolve and to change because once you hit your goal, you're going to want to go somewhere else. With that in mind the thing that works with most of these smaller groups that I'm in, the biggest thing is respect. We respect each other, we listen to each other, we enjoy each other and we try not to screw each other over on or off stage. With that we pass around the metaphorical conch, if you will.
>
> —*Bob Dassie*

This is fairly common among beginner start-up groups where, since all the members are equal in experience, no one steps up to lead. Group consensus is great for creating a safe environment for playing, since all hierarchies are removed, but it stunts growth since it is harder to mark progress without a leader. This structure works best with experienced players who wish to explore a particular approach or with practice groups where everyone wants to have an equal say.

Vision: Can vary based on experience. When everyone has an equal say, it can have a too-many-chefs quality. With more experienced players, it is usually the vision that initially brings them together and so the collaboration becomes more productive.

Artistic Growth: The ensemble will have some growth, but individuals will most likely not and will have to take care of themselves.

Personal Dynamic: Mixed bag. Everyone is on an equal level which makes for a more comfortable zone from which to generate ideas. Problems within the group, however, are tougher to address and rectify if there is no structure. Attempts to do so can undermine the commune-like feeling.

Sustainability: Many long-term groups with a lot of turnover tend to use this structure, but I suggest using this for the short-term if you must, and allow it to evolve into one of the other structures.

2. Group consensus with rotating directors.

Most groups that start with Structure 1 eventually feel the need to assign a leader. However, in keeping with the communal atmosphere, they decide to make the leadership temporary. This setup can work, provided that a director is allowed to have an effect on the troupe's overall performance. If you are assigning a different person to lead each rehearsal, then you are essentially hitting a reset button each time. Chances are the temporary director leads a lesson on one of the skill sets, something in which they are considered strong (e.g., character, physicality, etc.). One rehearsal (the average of which runs two to three hours) will hardly put a dent in the goal of the lesson, and the next time you meet you are already moving on. In addition, putting people in the position of critiquing each other can create tensions—where a leader's decision is suddenly undermined by another member based on something that happened during their lead. The result is a strengthening of basics with a toolbox of good ideas, but a stunting of growth similar to the previous structure, due to the lack of a sole vision. My suggestion to those whose troupe is set up this way is to alternate directors less frequently, possibly changing every month (preferably while taking time off from performing), to give each leader a chance to grow in the role. In turn, the progress will be easier to mark and a more solid vision will develop.

Vision: Will vary from project to project. When the directors are allowed to lead for longer, it will create a stronger foundation for the next director to build on rather than just having a collection of good ideas at the end of the month.

Artistic Growth: Individual abilities will be able to get more attention than the previous structure by building a big toolbox from which to work. The ensemble, however, will only be benefited by longer stretches of direction.

Personal Dynamic: There is still the personal tension of this dynamic but that can be lessened by the vocabulary you choose (mentioned later as "Creating a Safe Environment").

Sustainability: Short-term or long-term. This is helpful when your group has high turnover coupled with a regular performance venue.

3. Facilitating without directing.
Some groups have a facilitator rather than a director—someone who works from inside the group and makes sure certain things happen: rehearsals are organized, casting lists drawn up, etc. This occurs a lot with smaller groups who come together based on a common comfort level. Duties are divvied up, usually by one person who takes on a little more than the others. This dynamic can work, particularly in short-term projects or with small casts (2 – 4 people), but still greatly benefits from inviting an outside eye to coach on occasion.

Vision: The vision works by group consensus but is usually molded by the more aggressive members. Expect the central ideas to change often, like trends, rather than growing organically one from the other.

Artistic Growth: This depends on the boundaries that the facilitator draws for herself. Some facilitators assign the weekly leadership of the group or slate coaches. An organized person can help the group develop beyond the week-to-week needs.

Personal Dynamic: The focus is high on what makes the improvisation fun. The morale will be high but the professionalism may suffer.

Sustainability: To move to a long-term situation, an outside eye is helpful.

4. Directing and performing with the same group.

This is the most-used structure for groups in smaller markets where the improv community hasn't grown enough to provide the opportunity to direct outside one's own group, or perform outside the group under someone else's direction. This is also the dynamic for self-starters—for those who have a show they wish to create and end up running it as well as performing in it (the central reason for creating the show).

Vision: With one voice guiding, it is far easier to establish a strong vision for the show.

Artistic Growth: The director's performance will suffer, unless he is sufficiently experienced. It is also difficult to monitor other people's performances objectively from inside the improvisation.

Personal Dynamic: The added task of noting from within a show works against the noting process, while causing personal issues to enter the group dynamic if the right vocabulary is not in place. If this path is unavoidable, it is suggested that you focus solely on directing at first and allow the show to get on its feet for the first couple of shows. Similar to giving a skateboard a few good pushes before hopping on, it is a good idea to let the project develop some momentum of its own before entering as a performer.

Sustainability: Short-term or long-term, though it is exponentially harder the more members there are in the group.

5. Solely directing.

This is the dynamic I prefer most, especially when I have many projects running and can choose to not be involved in all aspects of each project. Taking on the role of sole director allows you to give more focused attention to all aspects of the show, including tech and music.

Vision: Strongest of all the structures. With a backbone in place that is uncomplicated by the director performing, the concept is able to solidify.

Artistic Growth: This is the strongest dynamic for bringing across a vision, because you lose the distractions of being a performer in the show.

Personal Dynamic: This varies depending on the personality of the director, but the maintenance is easier when there is a clear delineation between director and performer.

Sustainability: Can be sustained indefinitely, or at least until the director needs to pull out and focus on other projects.

DIRECTING VERSUS COACHING AND TEACHING

Coaching is about helping people through their things. When you're coaching a team, you're taking them as they are and you're trying to make them better.

—*Kevin Mullaney*

The field of improvisation has grown so much in the last twenty years, particularly in the larger cities of Chicago, New York and Los Angeles, that there has been a higher demand for artistic leadership. With this demand has come the new designation of coach.

The biggest difference between coaches and directors is the relationship between them and the group. A director's relationship is driven by his artistic vision first and foremost. The goals of the show are imposed onto the performers who are molded to pick from a specific set of choices. Performers in a musical improv show will learn to extend the moment into a song. Those doing improvised Shakespeare will play with archetypes common to the style. The coach, however, is there only to further the voice of the group rather than to impose their own ideals, adding new ideas to their tool box without making them dogma. The focus is to make the show polished, to minimize the margin of error, but without dictating approach or philosophy.

While this book offers many ideas applicable to the coach, it is written with the director in mind—someone who has a higher personal stake in the final product. This is not to say that coaches are lackadaisical about their job. They are as committed as anyone, but to an idea that is not their own. Bringing across these grander ideas is what we will further touch upon in later chapters.

...The first thing [Viola Spolin] said when I asked her to teach was "Teaching is a cleansing." And I finally understood what she meant. And that is when you teach even though you have taught the work time and time and time again, it keeps presenting a problem that is brand new, first time you've seen it because it's the first time it's been encountered by your student. And if you come with a bunch of history, or "I know how to solve this because I've solved this before," then you start getting jaded. I understood that the act of teaching is as much a discovery as the act of playing it.

—*Gary Schwartz*

The differences between directing and teaching are more than the obvious differences that come to mind. The biggest difference is the *purpose* that the attendees feel. A student has paid to be there and in doing so is giving a certain authority to you.

Another major factor is the way by which progress is gauged. As a director, you have a standard that you wish to meet with every show and to push the cast past. In classes, however, the students are their own gauges. They give when they can or want and may react adversely to being pushed. I have had students with no acting aspirations whatsoever who were looking to experience new things or improve other aspects of their life, or were in a vocation that could be enhanced with improv skills (public speakers, lawyers, etc.). Knowing this, I prioritize what to push in the students differently from how I might lead a rehearsal. Public speakers do not need to explore a variety of characters but they do need to command the stage. Lawyers do not need to work emotion as much as listening. Laymen looking to explore new hobbies will have to act out scenes alongside actors who are more versatile. These average Joes will need to learn to get from point A to point B in a scene without dealing with all the nuances that an actor would keep an eye on.

FOLLOWING THE BALL

When basketball coaches are watching the team play from the sidelines, they are urging the players on, while also keeping track of skills that need work, and the individual achievements and hiccups of each player. That is a lot to take stock of all at once, which is exactly how it can be for an improv director watching a scene. What helps guide the basketball coach is that above all he is following the ball. Regardless of how well the players are moving, blocking, etc., none of this matters if the ball doesn't go in the basket. A game, after all, is decided on points.

Though improv scenework has no point structure to dictate the goals

11

of the scene, there is a focus similar to the passing of a ball that guides the improv. (Even in competition-based formats like ComedySportz or Theatresports, there is something more than the achievement of one team over the other, a device for the audience and not the players.) What the focus is depends on you as director, and that focus can change from scene to scene.

Some think that when playing a specific game, the rules of the game are the focus (i.e., in Questions, how you only ask questions, in Sit Stand Kneel, one person must be in one of those positions at every point of the scene) but it is a focus that undercuts the fullest potential of the improv.

Going back to the basketball analogy, basketball as a *game* consists of passing, shooting, blocking, etc. but the *skill set* consists of speed, awareness, stamina and so on. In an improv scene, you can have the *game* of one-upsmanship between the two characters which employs the *skill set* of listening, character and environment.

So, how is the scene that you are watching progressing? What is the scene about? When there is a question as to what the ball is that we are following, look at what the characters commit to most emotionally. That is where the drive is for the characters and thus is the drive for the scene.

I recently saw a scene about a rivalry between two furniture makers where a third character came in to buy out one of the rivals and make it easier on the other. It wasn't a horrible choice but it didn't come from anything that the scene had established in the two minutes prior to that entrance. The entrance was done skillfully in that there was a clear character who was presented straightforwardly. The game, however, was interrupted. Being unconnected, the momentum stopped and then started up again, following a new storyline. In this case, the ball was moving when the scene focused on the rivalry. Once that was gone, there was nowhere to go; the ball was dropped.

STRIVING TO BE UNIQUE

I've worked with some teachers where they love throwing out fancy words to say the same thing that they could do with regular language. I think it's a way of making their ideas seem more important and I just like to keep it as simple and accessible as possible because I know when I learn things, that's how I want it to be. It's just like tell me what you're trying to tell me and let me see if I understand.

—Mark Sutton

In one of my directing classes, I was leading a notes session, where one half of the class would note the other and give them challenges. One of the students gave another the challenge to "find his character by looking into his scene partner's eyes." I asked him what he meant. He repeated it without elaboration but did mention that it was an idea he had used with his own troupe.

Just as players can sabotage themselves by going for the joke, directors can sabotage themselves by striving for the unique. My student's challenge was rather abstract, even though it felt concrete to him. It also smacked of a forced unique voice.

It is very common for directors to go through phases where we concoct fanciful theories in search of the right one. We are also players after all—usually—and are looking to break down how we play and how we "should" play. We feel a need to make our own sense of things. In this regard, improvisation has become like a religion, a spiritual center through which to relate.

When we forcefully strive to be unique, we are no longer fulfilling our purpose, which is to guide the group. Just as going for the joke at the expense of the scene is selfish, so is trying to make yourself look like a brilliant guru at the expense of real guidance. Your focus should always be on the group you are leading, rather than the specifics of what you are leading them through.

Teachers should teach what they believe is strongest...not the only way, but there are all these different aspects that you can learn. Each [teacher] has a strength and a tool that they use and they're all valuable and it gives you a weapon or a tool that you can use each time you go out.

—Jeff Griggs

I was transformed the day I sat in on a Mick Napier workshop. It was my first trip to Chicago and until then I thought I had a strong understanding of improvisation and "what not to do." I had just started directing at this point and was very focused in my criticism. I was also very much in the don't-ask-questions and quickly-establish-who-what-where mindset. This is a perfectly acceptable way to approach scenes but it is only one way. In one two-hour session led by Mick, I saw more options.

His entire workshop consisted of nothing but one-minute scenes, after which he would tell the players his observations. These usually pointed out where the actor checked out or made some other change brought about by self-inflicted obligations (e.g., the scene needs to go this way, my character needs to have a transformation here).

It was amazing how much could be learned from only one minute of scenework. That is because all the key decisions are made within the first minute of a scene; in fact, they could probably be found in the first five seconds. Regardless of what format or length of form you are playing with, keep in mind that the scene is still your basic building block. How that block breaks down further depends upon the lens you are training on it and the needs of the approach you are pursuing. It could be scenework based on premise, character, narrative or any of the other aspects of improv (there is a thorough list enclosed in the chapter on creating improv formats with your troupe). What you choose at this level will define you as a director and teacher. One thing that I asked of all the directors I interviewed for this book is what was the first thing that they taught new improvisers. The answers varied from conveying the idea of having fun to showing the fundamentals of creating a character on stage. What is the first thing you would teach?

GETTING OUT OF THE WAY

This the biggest part of any director's job—and the hardest. We want so much for the performance to go right and for the players to make the right choices. We become concerned parents who overprotect our children. And as with overprotective parents, there is a danger of being stifling. We interrupt scenes, we correct choices, and even call out moves to be made as a moment unfolds. Nothing can grow under those conditions—especially not instincts.

> Ultimately, you can just kind of guide people to more empowering choices and it's up to them to be able to take them on. You can't get into the mistake of trying to reshape them...It's this whole idea of you invite them into trying to work on a bad habit or change a skill or try something new. Then, ultimately, they have to choose to do it or they don't. You can give them some

encouragement and support to make it easier, but if you become a crusader about it you're just going to make it tough for both of you guys."

—Armando Diaz

As a result, a line sometimes gets crossed between guiding choices and dictating them—the first is sidecoaching and the latter is what I call "choicecoaching." Choicecoaching happens when we focus our sights too narrowly on the minutiae of the improvisation rather than keeping a watch on the bigger picture. After all, that particular scene will never happen again. That moment where the one player *should have* kissed the other, or *should have* used the gun, or *should have* reincorporated that information from her history from earlier in the scene—that specific alignment of plot elements—will not occur again. What will come up again is the type of choices that player makes—tenative, forced, surreal, etc.—and the personal issues that push them in that direction; but directors who watch the scene as if they were a performer can't see that. They instead look at what they would have done in the scene. But you are not in the scene and while your tendencies suit you, they do not automatically suit anybody else.

I have been choicecoached in a scene and I can tell you while at the end of it my fellow players and I felt like it was a good scene, it was the equivalent of empty calories. All the great choices, the choice to confront the other character, the choice to interrupt the two lovers who were about to come together for the laugh—all these choices were not mine. I was being used to play out what the director would have done were they in the scene themselves. I felt used and did not feel particularly good about my own skills since I did not get to use them in that scene.

> To a certain extent you may think you're the actors' boss but the actors are really the ones in charge because they're the ones doing it. How do you get Actor A to understand or to get that making this kind of choice is his idea, so that it's organic. If you're just telling them what to do, in the purest sense of that, if you're just saying "well you should've done this, that and the other thing," then you're just giving them trivia.
>
> *—Dan O'Connor*

The job of the improv director is far simpler than we make it out to be. As a director, I can show my cast exercises and opportunities. I can give my observations on their work and how it is progressing. I can show them a direction in which to go, an avenue to explore. I cannot, however, change them. I can illuminate and illustrate; the rest is up to them.

CHAPTER 2: BREAKING DOWN THE WORK

Improvisation is a personal artform and everyone has their "way" to approach it. The way is influenced by their own comfort levels, their personal experiences and whatever school of thought they have been exposed to. However, regardless of whether you follow Spolin or Close or Johnstone, whether you've studied theater or law, whether you are performing in a bar or on television, there are several commonalities.

CHOICES AND COMMITMENTS

Del Close talked about finding the game of the scene. Keith Johnstone describes establishing the who, what and where early on. Whether your final goal is to create narrative or heighten a moment, you are still focusing on a type of choice that you must sustain.

Improvisation, for all its technique and complexities, can still be broken down into these two acts: making a choice and committing to that choice. The fact that your philosophy differs from those of the players you are directing should not affect your ability to lead them. Instead, you can look at how they play within their own framework. Do they make their choices right away? Do they stay neutral and then discover a choice? Do they base their choices solely on their partner's choice, avoiding initiative in a scene? These are all questions that are distinct from whatever the underlying improv theory is.

The idea of commitment can equally be looked at from an objective distance. Does the player back down from her choice in the presence of her partner's choices? Does she tend to make multiple choices in quick succession or does she stick with one choice for a long time? (Either answer could signal an issue or a benefit, depending on the context of the scene being observed.)

If we look at the underlying issues in a person's work, we can then avoid being bogged down by philosophies and their semantics.

THE IMPROV IS BIGGER THAN YOU

At the Hothouse we use a term called "predator mind," a hyper-awareness of the external. Athletes call it the zone. A predator has no time to worry about itself else it will miss its next meal. It stays in a state of active waiting, Spolin calls this no motion. The moment that stick breaks in the brush the predator heads straight for it, no questions asked. When we improvise we are constantly scanning the space for inspiration, waiting for that "stick to break." The "food" of the scene. Gotta feed the Beast. The Beast will tell you what it wants to eat—you just have to listen.

—Todd Stashwick

Todd comes from a background influenced heavily by Spolin and the organic improv techniques of Shira Piven, but all schools share in the idea that there is the equivalent of a god that hangs over the performance. Del Close even held invocations to help tap into this greater power. Whether it is the beast, group mind, the game—to a certain degree, even the laugh— there is an aspiration to connect, with the other performers and with the audience. Sometimes, as in many clowning-influenced philosophies, there is an attempt to connect with one's own true self.

Simultaneous with these goals is the acknowledgement, maybe conscious, maybe unconscious, that the individual is dwarfed by the entity. Whatever the level of strength of an actor's improvisational ability, it is still only a contribution to something larger. The definition of this thing is up to you. Most likely you are going to pull from one of the pre-existing ideas from Spolin, Del, Johnstone, Annoyance, etc. and that is perfectly wonderful. Picking one school of thought to work from is like when someone opens a business and decides whether to be a not-for-profit or a for-profit corporation. It does not dictate what the business will be, but how it will be organized. There are thousands of people who have studied under Del Close or under his closest disciples. Each of them are doing different types of performances.

Those who try to create their own definition of what the work *truly* is will find they are still derivative of what came before, except now they have made it more complicated. There is a reason why the philosophies of the "masters" have lasted as long as they have; it is because they have touched upon the simplest, purest essence of what they get from the work. Even Picasso painted traditional portraits for many years before focusing on Cubism—an idea that he gleaned from Cezanne's work, then explored further.

IMPROV SHORTHAND

Like any artform or vocation, improvisation has a vocabulary associated with it. The game, the scene, the get, and the out are some of the terms that come up in improv discussions. The terms developed in isolation for many years, causing a Tower of Babel effect whenever improvisers from different backgrounds came together. Many of the games and exercises that we all use are known under different names. What one group calls *Hesitation*, another calls *What Happens Next* or *Caller's Option* or *Director* or *Interrupted Scene*. Warm-ups of the same name often have different instructions that are given as, over the years, new variations are created and then passed on as the original.

Similarly, the various aspects of improvisation and scenework get grouped under different headings. For instance, the term "relationship" has been used to describe the logistical relationship between two characters such as brothers, lovers, or employer and employee, as well as the emotional relationship (i.e., A is scared of B, B is in love with A, etc.) Eventually, I learned to employ the shorthand term "dynamic" to relay the latter idea, a term I define anew with each group I instruct.

All these labels are secondary to the idea behind them, which should not suffer because of semantics. Be prepared when leading a workshop or rehearsal to set and define certain terms at the beginning and repeat them continually as you develop the voice for yourself and the group.

THE ARC

Every show, scene, monologue, and song has an arc to it with a beginning, middle and end—even if you want nothing to do with narrative. Even if you do nothing in your scene but sit in a chair for three minutes and stare blankly at the audience, there is an arc. If there wasn't, how would we know when the scene was done?

An arc is a transport from one idea to another, no matter how small the idea. Many equate the transformation of a character with the arc, that once the audience has seen a change, the scene is over. This is only one way to go. Vladimir and Estragon, the main characters in *Waiting for Godot*, go through a two-act journey of events and end up exactly where they started, no transformation for better or worse. What has changed is the audience's perception of the two. Didi and Gogo go on and on about their boredom, their lack of progress and their desire to die. So when after the two acts have passed and our protagonists haven't acheived anything, the audience understands that their lives have always been, and will always be like this—static. With this realization, the audience gains or loses sympathy for the characters. That is an arc.

Finding what the arc is of any given scene—whether it is driven by plot, emotion, or any other pattern—helps you better direct the editing between the scenes and the calls of your lighting person.

TRAINING WHEELS

There are a number of rules that have been applied to improv. Ideas about not asking questions and saying "Yes And" and not doing transaction scenes and making your partner look good. You may not agree with some or any of these examples but you recognize them and the dozens of others like them that you have encountered in your classes and rehearsals. We are taught that improv is the artform of limitless possibilities, yet we have to couple it with not being able to say "no."

Rather than looking at these guidelines as rules, I see them as training wheels. The difference is that, eventually, training wheels can be taken off. Improvisations are representations of realistic moments of life and our lives are filled with significant, interesting scenes where someone told us no or we had a transaction with a cashier we didn't know. So why do these rules come up?

When instructors push to not ask questions, what they are trying to say is that a scene is easier to build with statements. Transaction scenes are bypassed because characters with a shared history provide a more fertile ground for developing the relationship. These training wheels are extremes applied to scenework to help the players make stronger choices (we will discuss working with extremes in *Giving Notes and Challenges*). Somehow, along the way, these ideas became law and many new directors pass them on without an understanding of what is behind it.

When you come across these rules, look into the behavior it is trying to prevent and consider whether that is a concern for the group of people you are working with. The level of performers I play with tend to have no trouble conveying information in their scenes, whether they are asking questions or not (there is even a game where all you can do is ask questions, so how detrimental can they really be?).

****

Along the way you are going to come across improvisers with radically different mindsets of what "good" improv looks like. Finding the common ground among your students will make it a lot easier for you to open them up to what you have to show. In the end, you will have broadened their range along the way and broadened your own as a teacher.

CHAPTER 3: GIVING NOTES AND CHALLENGES

> If you negate your intelligence or you negate your responsibility as the passionate observer, then I think you've really let your cast down. They're counting on you to give the feedback and that can be supportive. You don't have to be an asshole. You don't have to be an autocrat. You don't have to be a cretin about it. You have to be honest; you have to be fair, while at the same time encouraging. Sometimes, you give them a little sugar with the slap or whatever.
>
> —*Michael Gellman*

Improvisation is the most personal of all the performance arts. Performers without a script to guide their actions and motivations tend to pull a lot from their own lives and personalities. This can create tension and defensiveness to a director's notes because, to a player, critiques on the scene choices they've made can feel personal.

This is why some directors are particular about their phrasing or presentations of notes. Rather than address an issue with one individual, they will bring it up as if it is something the whole troupe should work on. Some directors will "cushion the blow" of a bad note by making sure to start with a positive note. They are concerned that they will make the improviser feel bad, preventing them from doing their best work. To that end, they attempt to create an environment where "everything is okay." This can ring false and actually taint the environment as a result. The players know when there is one person who is lagging behind and feel it when they have to take on their burden with extraneous notes. They feel the rhythm of your direction and will spend the time during their positive notes waiting for the other shoe to drop with a "but..." which will defeat the purpose of the good note. The way to provide a safer environment for the improvisers is not by altering the presentation of the notes but the intent behind them. This means reevaluating what we directors are looking to accomplish with our notes, or as we will start to call them, challenges.

The choices that improvisers make on stage are usually in line with the choices they make in life—or the exact opposite. So pointing out these problems in their work doesn't always guarantee a turnaround. In fact, sometimes, it can worsen the situation by making the player more self-conscious about his deficiencies.

Let's look at the (unfortunately) rather common note: "You need to get out of your head." If there's one thing that will get an improviser more in his head, it's pointing out that they are already there. What we need to do as directors, instead of spotlighting the player's weakness, is to give them a challenge to focus on that will force them into other choices. Challenge them to make constant physical contact with their scene partner, for example. This forces a choice at the start of the scene without giving them time to think about it. Furthermore, the forced contact creates an automatic relationship with their scene partner's character. Either they are hanging on to them out of adoration, or out of a desperate need for protection, or a hundred other justifications that can provide grounding for a scene.

Challenges work best when they are dramatic extremes that allow the actors to feel an immediate difference in their work without being sidetracked by the methodology behind it. At the gym, people test and push their limits. They bench-press 200-pound weights, not because they are walking around in their everyday lives lifting 200-pound objects but because it makes it easier to lift all things. Similarly, playing extremes allows the actors to raise the bar on all their skills.

I, myself, have had to overcome the hurdle of not being able to emote on stage, which was directly related to how I was in life. Slowly, I began to discover shortcuts to conveying emotions on stage that I have used to help others with the same issue. For instance, a player who is having trouble emoting could use the Distance Challenge. For this challenge they need to think of a specific distance at the top of each scene and maintain that distance from their partner for the *entire* scene. This challenge works if the distance chosen is as specific as possible, whether it's three inches or three yards. As a result of just picking a distance, the player's cadence will change, their inflection will change and, through those things, they will convey emotion. A cheat sheet of challenges appears later in this chapter.

In creating a challenge for a player, be aware of their patterns. Most improvisers have defaults they play under, sometimes to the point of being a crutch, doing that which is comfortable or what is known to "work." The best way to grow in this artform is to recognize these patterns and learn to break them. The best improvisers are able to play under any conditions, in any format and in any style. It is a matter of having the choices come from the moment or the character and not from the actor in an attempt at self-preservation.

Breaking out of patterns is not always about finding problems or things that need to be fixed. Let's face it: you couldn't change someone if you wanted to—you can only illustrate new ideas to them. Also, you will create a tense working environment if your direction is solely about "correcting" people. Those players getting the breadth of the notes will get self-conscious about their work. Meanwhile, your stronger players are going to get bored, since they're not being challenged and will resent those players who might be holding their progress back.

Identify patterns as an objective observation, devoid of judgment as to whether they are "bad" patterns or "good" patterns. Some aspects of the work, after all, can be judged either way. There is an improviser with whom I have worked who was very good at establishing environment in scenes. This can be considered a positive note of his work. However, the player would start the majority of his scenes with an environment-based initiation, sometimes to the point of not being aware of his scene partner until after the completion of his opening physical gambit.

Any asset valuable to improvisation can also be used in a detrimental way. If the audience sees that great character one time too many, or that sure-fire narrative structure one more time, they will start to turn on you, regardless of how often it has worked in the past. We should aim to give the audience something as original as possible every single time we step out on stage.

When we remove judgment from our observations we can also tend to the needs of our stronger players, giving them new areas to explore and help them broaden their range.

In order to keep the challenges from becoming or appearing subjective, avoid using negations in your directions (i.e., don't, no, or not). Players do better work when they can explore rather than focus on limitations. Or, as The Annoyance Theater in Chicago puts it, improvisers should play out of inspiration, not obligation. Instead of noting your players to not ask questions, challenge them to talk in exclamation marks. There may be multiple patterns that you would want to address, but for now let's focus on helping the player through one at a time.

CREATING CHALLENGES

This will require patience and determination in your role as director. Here are some questions to help guide you in giving notes:

1. What patterns do I see in the player's work? These patterns have to do with either the types of choices they tend to make or the types of choices they tend to commit to.

2. If I don't see patterns, what things has the performer done that I'd like them to further explore? This will help broaden their range, particularly the nuances.

3. What extreme can I challenge them to that will affect that pattern or make them explore that angle? For rehearsals, it is perfectly acceptable to give specific challenges (a chart is shown below to aid you). Rehearsals are, after all, the place where you can experiment freely.

Patterns are most easily recognized when the players are asked to do a succession of quick scenes, approximately one minute in length. (Note: these are scenes that do not aim to be one minute long but are edited after one minute.) Have the players do a series of one-minute open scenes where they apply these challenges. Allow for a few scenes to pass before giving any feedback on the work. The effects of any given challenge are more easily recognized after the players have had a chance to play its range.

CHALLENGES CHEAT SHEET

Here is list of focuses that one would like to impose on the players and sample challenges that might help achieve that.

Looking to put the focus on	Challenge
Big Choices	Bad Celebrity Impression, Extreme Mask
Brevity or Focus	Dialogue Spelling, Dynamic Pose, Fixed Gaze
Connection with Scene Partner	Constant Physical Contact, Distance Challenge, Last Line Repeat

Consistency of Character	Dynamic Pose, Fixed Gaze, Unspoken Object
Emotion	Distance Challenge, Extreme Mask
Environment	Hitting the Mark
High Status Characters	Shakespearean Challenge
Initiative	Constant Physical Contact, Extreme Mask, Making Noise
Low Status Characters	Dialogue Spelling, Last Line Repeat
Physicality	Bad Celebrity Impression, Constant Physical Contact
Relationship	Constant Physical Contact, Distance Challenge
Slowing Down	Dynamic Pose, Fixed Gaze
Vocal Variety	Musical Instrument

Bad Celebrity Impression

The challenge: The key to this challenge is doing a *bad* impression of the celebrity as if that person were improvising a scene rather than making the scene about any of the specifics of that person's life or work. If, for example, you are portraying Marilyn Monroe, you would incorporate the breathy talk and the sultry movement rather than the dress blowing up or quotes from *Some Like It Hot*. The focus is strictly on the mannerisms and worldview of the personality being imitated.

The effects: This challenge is one I learned from Joe Bill of Chicago's Annoyance Theater, his intention being to get the players to make out-of-the-ordinary character choices. When the players aim to do the impression badly, they tend to lose the censors in their heads that would force them to "do things right" and will also play their choices bigger. Regardless of whether or not they do spot-on imitations, they will undoubtedly do their most varied character work.

Constant Physical Contact

The challenge: Player for the duration of each scene makes constant physical contact with their scene partner. This should be automatic at the top of the scene, without any need for justification.

The effects: By making physical contact, the player is forcing the relationship to an extreme such as adoration or servitude. This challenge also helps a player who you feel might be in their head. The choice the improviser is forced to make is extreme, as is the commitment required by making it a challenge of constant contact. The player's focus instantly becomes heightened on their scene partner and the relationship between them.

Dialogue Spelling

The challenge: Ptolemy Slocum, of The Peoples Improv Theater, introduced this idea to me during a coaching session where the players had to spell out every word in every line of dialogue they spoke. For example: I-L-O-V-E-Y-O-U. For added difficulty, he would have the players spell out the punctuation (as in I-L-O-V-E-Y-O-U-C-O-M-M-A-M-O-M), but I prefer this as a variation.

The effects: A person's dialogue becomes more concise the more effort the player has to put into each line. Exposition gets minimized. Filler gets removed completely. The player does more with less. One thing to watch for is that there are still complete sentences, as opposed to "caveman speak" where one noun is passed off as a full thought.

Distance Challenge

The challenge: The player needs to think of a specific distance at the top of each scene and maintain that distance from his partner for the ENTIRE scene, picking a new distance for each scene. This challenge works if the distance chosen is as specific as possible, whether it's three inches or three yards.

The effects: Picking a distance forces a relationship based on one character's attitude toward the other. The character now has a compulsion to stay away or keep close to the other. This creates an immediate two-person dynamic and is a great shortcut for conveying emotions.

Dynamic Pose

The challenge: Player begins each scene by freezing in a dynamic pose—dynamic meaning as much of the body that can be engaged at once. The player holds this pose for the duration of the scene down to the way the head is being held. If, for example, they have their head tilted upward, then it is preferred that they not feel the need to adjust so as to better see their scene partner. It says more about the relationship if the two characters are consistently not making eye contact because one of them is focused elsewhere.

The effects: I use the Dynamic Pose when I want a player to be less frenetic and more focused. By limiting the player's movement and focusing them on committing to a strong choice at the top of the scene, it helps those who adapt very quickly to their partner's offers while dropping their own offers as well as those who are highly aggressive about creating scenic activity.

Dynamic Pose—Slide Show Variation

The challenge: This variation allows the player to move, as long as he moves into another dynamic pose and holds it. I often encourage the players to aim for as few poses as possible. Anytime an improviser increases his limitations it can increase their exploration.

The effects: The variation helps players make stronger, more potent offers while keeping the narrative simple.

Extreme Mask

The challenge: Player begins each scene with a "mask" which requires contorting as much of the face as possible. The eyebrows and mouth are the key components to watch.

The effects: Masks create very stylized characters, almost Commedia-like, with consistent emotions and/or attitudes. A face with a huge snarl will never be happy, while a face with a huge smile will never get angry. Some find that an extreme enough mask has an effect on their entire physicality.

Fixed Gaze

The challenge: The player keeps his gaze fixed on a specific point in the environment or on his scene partner.

The effects: This is another example of a challenge meant to keep a character grounded in a situation, particularly if he hinges a lot of what he does on what the partner does. You can see this when they are making constant eye contact with their partner. A person who is constantly focused on the heavens or a spot offstage in the distance will produce a certain type of personality with a certain view of the world. An improviser who is challenged to keep his gaze fixed somewhere on or around the scene partner will create stronger status dynamics each time. Someone who is constantly staring at your crotch will have a different relationship with you than someone who is staring at your feet or six inches past your left ear. Remember, the more specific the choices, the more heightened they will be, making it easier for the actors to commit to their choices.

Hitting the Mark

The challenge: Before doing a string of scenes, hand the player a roll of masking tape. Ask him to place five pieces on the floor anywhere on the stage area. Those then become the improviser's marks which they are to hit during the scenes. Make sure the actor varies how many marks he hits from scene to scene or in what order. Challenge him to hit as few marks as possible, or to hit only a couple over and over again.

The effects: The marks are good for players who aren't connected to their environment, who perform activities in nebulous space. It can also help those who are frenetic players to be more focused. Instead of moving all over the stage they will confine themselves to specific areas. These areas will then develop a special significance as a result.

Last Line Repeated

The challenge: The player must repeat the line of his scene partner before every line of his own dialogue. For example:

A: This is the nicest date I ever had.

B: This is the nicest date I ever had. We are so lucky to have found each other!

or

A: This is the nicest date I ever had.

B: Ever had? But I'll bet you've gone on hundreds of dates.

The effect: A player becomes more aware of his partner's offer and more readily builds from it. This also helps those who are often driving scenes to learn back-seat roles.

Making Noise

The challenge: Player begins each scene with a sound. These sounds should be sounds that people normally make in life—such as laughing, sighing, sucking through teeth, etc.—as opposed to sound effects.

The effects: Making a noise at the top of the scene helps those with trouble initiating. A noise is an easy choice to commit to and isn't hard to come up with. An added bonus is that the character that is created will tend to have a more focused and consistent point of view. If the scene is lacking that consistency, sidecoach the player to repeat the sound throughout.

Musical Instrument

The challenge: Player imitates different musical instruments with his voice in each scene. The idea is to mimic the style of sound each produces in their words. Imitating a flute might create a shrill, hyper character voice while a tuba will inspire a slow-talking, sullen voice.

The effects: Making an instrumental choice can make for unusual voice-based characters that go beyond doing accents. It affects the cadence of their speech and, in turn, their character's attitude.

Shakespearean Challenge

The challenge: Player maneuvers through each scene as if they were in a Shakespearean play. The focus is on the movement of the Shakespearean performer rather than Shakespearean speech or content. Keep an eye on varying the character types, from playing kings to fools, lovers to deceivers.

The effects: Similar to the Bad Celebrity Impression challenge, this eliminates the internal censors and allows for bigger out-of-the-ordinary character choices. More specifically, it focuses the improvisers on more high-status choices even when playing lower roles.

Talking in Exclamation Points
The challenge: Player ends every line of dialogue with an exclamation point. Watch that this does not result in the player simply making everything louder and faster. The emphasis should be about making the speech more impassioned. Every line is the most important thing that the character has to say at that moment.

The effects: This is another shortcut to emoting on stage. The added significance that is given to the dialogue will also get the improviser more grounded in the story of the scene because now they are more invested.

Unspoken Object
The challenge: Player begins each scene with a mimed object that remains unspoken. If the partner talks about the object or the activity she is involved in, they should be encouraged to change the subject. A sidecoach that helps is challenging the player to make a "you are" statement. When the improviser states something like "You are destroying our friendship" or "You are the best worker I have ever seen," it makes the scene about the relationship rather than about the activities, which are just garnish.

The effects: Having an object in hand helps ground characters who might otherwise fade in and out. A female character who smokes from a long cigarette holder has a specific feel to it, as does a person who is constantly cleaning a gun. Or a child who will not put down her cat's cradle. Make sure that the player explores miming objects of different sizes and weights. Interesting side note: In all the times I have used this challenge there are three objects that come up the most: 1) cigarette, 2) beverage, usually alcoholic, and 3) yo-yo, believe it or not, to play children.

CREATING YOUR OWN CHALLENGES

You cannot teach by rote, you have to teach by intuition…you gotta get it in your bones. That's number one. Then you gotta be a diagnostician. Number two, you have to figure out what's going on with that person. And then not tell him what's going on, but try to figure out what game or what side coach would solve his problem.

—*Gary Schwartz*

30

Creating challenges comes in two stages: identifying patterns and then finding an extreme to break the patterns. If you're having difficulty coming up with suitable challenges consider this:

if not _____, then _____.

If I want my actor to be less focused on environment, then what should they be focused on instead? If we want them to explore character more, could we use the "extreme mask" challenge? If we want more of a focus on relationship, would the constant physical contact challenge or the distance challenge work? Think of specific examples of scenes that would satisfy what you are looking to see and find an extreme aspect that the improviser could play.

For example, the anatomy of using the Shakespearean challenge to create a higher-status character followed this train of thought: What characteristics would you assign to a person who is high status? Their physical stature is straight, their movement is focused and specific, and they have a loud and commanding voice. What characters or genre of characters also share these qualities? From there the idea of Shakespearean influences on a scene makes sense.

Other things to consider are whether this is a clear objective for the player, and how best to communicate it to the player. Shakespeare is a universally understood style of theater even to those not involved in entertainment (thus the success of characters like Jon Lovitz' Master Thespian). The idea of playing a scene in a Shakespearean way should evoke an immediate image of what that looks like to any improviser, so the objective is clear. In communicating we want the actor to focus on the movement aspect of the genre without the use of the Shakespearean dialogue or content (i.e., seeing your father's ghost, plotting a deception against the king, etc.). Putting limitations on a scene is difficult without using negative words, but as long as the main thrust of your challenge is on the positive goal, the negative limitations won't feel negative. For example:

"I want you to do the next few scenes where you move like a Shakespearean character. The focus is on the movement rather than using Shakespearean style dialogue or plot points."

In the anatomy of getting to the challenge, I listed a commanding voice as one of the characteristics that would help establish higher status characters, but did not refer to it in the challenge. This is because the various aspects of the work are interdependent. By affecting the players' physicality, we will affect the tone and resonance of their voice. Changes may also occur in the challenged player's story choices, emotional choices, and how they use the stage. It is an artistic version of trickle-down theory.

The key for a director is to build with the improviser from one point outward; rather than trying to affect every aspect at once, make one adjustment and see what other effects it has.

APPLYING AND MODIFYING CHALLENGES

> We don't allow people to say no that's wrong onstage so we shouldn't as teachers be there to say, "No you did that wrong." What you're saying is "I didn't know that you could do that," and you have to be willing to say, "Hmm, you just taught me something," and be able to allow that to influence you and for you to learn from your students and move forward.
>
> —*Jeff Griggs*

In giving the challenges, you can refrain from even mentioning the desired result of the challenge as was done in the Shakespearean challenge given above. This helps keep the player from being focused on the end result rather than being in the moment. Also, there will be occasions when the challenge may result in an unexpected outcome. This will allow you to modify the challenge and retain progress in the direction of that player.

The challenges should be played a few scenes in a row without comment. The difference in the work will be evident to the performer, though may not be what you had intended in issuing the challenge. Even if this is the case, dramatic results will emerge for you to build from.

As you go through scenework with the challenges applied, you may find a need to adjust the challenge given because:

- The player has misunderstood the challenge.

- The change in their work is different from or is the complete opposite of the result expected.

- The resulting change in the pattern is too subtle.

The first thing to note is whether there is any change whatsoever, once again removing judgment of whether it is a good or bad change. Remember, as a director you can introduce new ideas to your players, but the effect they have is up to them. Therefore, any change that comes up is a positive result of your notes.

Improvisers also progress at different rates, especially when it comes to breaking deeply ingrained habits. My own habit of underemoting is a project that I have been working on for a while. There are lessons that I still need to refresh myself on from time to time.

I sometimes run performers through a gauntlet where they do a string of consecutive unrelated scenes with different partners from the group using the same challenge each time. This helps loosen up the improviser further, keeping them from planning ahead too much for the next scene and forcing them to make more unexpected choices.

If you are finding one player to be a particularly tough nut to crack, step up the specificity of your challenge. Let's say we challenge one actor to imitate an animal in each scene in order to introduce more character variety and physicality into their work. The improviser, however, seems to be holding back. The physicality is still minimal, with all movement occurring very close to the body.

First check with them on what specific animals he is imitating after each scene. This will indicate whether the issue is with the choice or the commitment level. If the player is choosing very similar and simple animals, the source is in the choices. If he is choosing varied inspirations that are not coming across, then he needs to commit more.

If it is the choice, focus him on new genres to play within, such as aquatic animals, to inspire more fluid movement; or larger animals to inspire bigger physicality. If you are looking to adjust his commitment levels, you can modify by quantifying the choices he has made. For instance, if the inspiration is a tiger, coach him by saying "That is a great tiger. On a scale of one to ten, it's at a five. Let's see what a ten tiger looks like." Intensifying a choice makes it easier for the player to not drop it.

Another option is a redo. Since we are working in one-minute scenes we can easily have the scenes replayed when necessary. This takes the focus off creating for the player and puts their focus on committing to the choices. Make sure the players understand that the replay is not a test to perfectly remember every little thing that was said or done but to give the same sense of the previous scene. If you are instructing the improvisers to do the scene a few times in a row you can add the challenge of doing the scene twice as fast or twice as long. Which version did they prefer? This will give you an insight into where the boundaries of their comfort zone lie and why they have a harder time committing to certain choices. You can also use the replay to add a second challenge to broaden their range in more than one aspect.

One thing to watch for is the improviser's need to justify the quirk that they are performing. A player stuck in a dynamic pose will feel the need to explain, in character, why they suddenly cannot move as opposed to letting it be a choice of the character to not move. These forced justifications (e.g., "I've gone and glued my feet to the floor," "I threw my back out," etc.) are the performer trying to be comfortable with something that feels wrong to do. Give the performer permission to never bring up the why and the scenic choices will be much stronger.

Challenges are also useful for those looking to direct themselves. Many times when we are doing a show we sit in judgment of ourselves when we are offstage. We tell ourselves things like, "My characters suck tonight" or, "This is my worst show ever." Obviously, these are not useful thoughts during a performance. Challenges can help focus a player on something that can be changed immediately and help him regain control over choices that he may have lost.

GIVING NOTES AFTER A SHOW

> When you give a penny lecture, the lecture comforts the teacher more than it does the student.
>
> —*Gary Schwartz (relaying Viola Spolin)*

If you are spending more than ten minutes on notes after a show then you are trying to do too much. The standard approach that many troupes default to is a scene-by-scene breakdown of the show immediately afterward, with an itemized list of "mistakes" that were made alongside a list of the "funny things" that happened. Allow me to suggest another way.

First, it helps if notes are not made immediately following the show. Emotions are highest, particularly on the night of a really bad show, and your players are anxiously awaiting the opportunity to talk to the friends they had in the audience. Instead, get them in a group and announce that they will have ten minutes to talk to their friends and arrange a place they can meet up with them afterwards. This break will also give those players who are especially down on their performance or the show as a whole the opportunity to talk with you privately to help vent some of those feelings. In certain cases you might wish to initiate the conversation yourself (grouping them for the announcement is a good way to get a reading of who might need this). The one-on-one will provide a safer environment for them to talk freely while allowing you control during the session.

Show notes are most effective when they look to the next performance or rehearsal. What were the strongest points of the show you just performed? What are the challenges for the next time? Sometimes I will simply ask the troupe I am directing, "Which scene did you have the most fun doing? Which scene do you think I had the most fun watching?" Rarely will the two answers be different. The fun is usually tied in with where they were the most connected, most confident, most playful or took the biggest risks. At the very least, it will show the types of scenes in which they are most comfortable.

Anything beyond those key observations can wait until the beginning of the next rehearsal or be integrated into the warm-ups for the next performance. Remember, there is only so much information that can be taken in at one time, particularly in such a vulnerable time as after a show. The more concise your notes, the better chance those notes have of sticking.

Specifics from the scenes should only be brought up to illustrate general observations. Why? Because while you feel that scene could have gone a different way or that character could have made a stronger choice, that set of circumstances will never come up again. Discussing what could have been in that moment won't do as much to give the players the tools they need in approaching future scenes.

Shortform shows will require more time as you will need to go over specific mechanics of the games in your set list. As a director, you want to group these notes as much as possible, rather than simply going in order through the set. This will help minimize redundancy. For example, Mad

Libs (a.k.a. Fill in the Blanks, Columns, etc.) is a scenic game where the players have pauses in their dialogue that the audience fills in. Puppets (a.k.a. Moving Bodies) is another scenic game where the players can only talk while audience volunteers serve as puppeteers manipulating their movements. These are two completely different games but ultimately both are about the immediate justification of audience input and working with volunteers on top of maintaining a good scene. Chances are I would group these games if I needed to note one of those aspects.

In your notes you can create headings, categories that they would fall under. Some examples would be Character, Narrative, Taking Care of the Audience, or Presentation. As you watch the show, fill in observations under the headings, creating new ones as necessary. This will help your direction in two ways. You will find a more balanced set of notes that includes both positive and negative observations. Having that balance will show your players what to strive for. (e.g., "The characters in Split Screen were emotionally the same, unlike in Jump Genre, where you had this great dynamic because of the emotional difference between them.") Secondly, it will help you prioritize your notes. Headings with the most thoughts listed are obviously more important to address. If you are keeping yourself to a strict time limit, you will find it easier to let certain notes go.

The following is a sample note sheet from a twenty-minute longform set. The headings reflect the issues that were being worked on in previous rehearsals—mainly a need to better maintain strong energy in scenes and playing with the timing and technique of scene editing. In addition, there would normally be a catch-all column, which has not been included here, for any comments that don't fall under either category but are worth noting.

	Energy	Edits
Joel	• playing with emotional openings more • good initiation of montage (phone calls)	• finding ends of scenes well
Jesse	• intense opening stances, makes for consistent characters • similar rhythms to characters	• finding ends of scenes well

Anita	• Still keeping arms folded, feels defensive, comes across as conflict • characters, while similar, are consistent. not dropping agendas	• hesitant on edits
Alec	• noncommittal supporting character (butler, frat boy)	• good reincorporating of Joel's montage as an editing device between beats
Dwayne	• High-status roles (dealer character) without agendas keeps energy low	• finding ends of scenes well
Erica	• starts with conflict each time. would be good to vary emotional energy	• sweep edits. experiment with other types of edit? • nice in how she did not rush offstage when edited, creating a theatrical overlap of scenes

These notes range from being subjective to objective since they are for my viewing only. Based on these observations, I would use the note session to point out the advances that have been made in communicating edits, pointing out specific instances from the show to illustrate and put forward a challenge to establish stronger energies at the top of scenes. There would also be side notes for Anita in regard to her default body language and how it is hindering her scenic choices. In the coming rehearsals I would give her a Dynamic Pose challenge to help her vary her opening physicality and mood.

The best time for challenges is as part of the warm-up before the next show. Based on the scenario above, I would focus on energy-building exercises such as Pass the Phrase or Superhero I (see Appendix) to get started, followed by running through as many opening lines for as many scenes as can be done in a minute. With this I acknowledge the good work of the previous set, while putting the focus squarely where it belongs—on the next show and what can be explored there.

CHAPTER 4: BUILDING AN ENSEMBLE

> Everything you do comes from responding to the other people on stage with you, and that is totally liberating. In improvisation the ensemble, in every sense, is your everything.
>
> —*Shira Piven*

As a director, you assume the responsibility of taking care of the group artistically. You are expected to keep an eye on the whole while not squashing the individuals. Unfortunately, the lines are blurry between being disciplined and domineering; between showing openness to ideas and spinelessness toward your own; between imposing your voice and molding that of the group.

CREATING A SPACE FOR IMPROV

> I think everything you believe about coaching an individual can be extended metaphorically to coaching an ensemble as one large, schizophrenic, moody individual.
>
> —*Jill Bernard*

We are responsible for the atmosphere in which the improv is done. Are we creating a playful "anything goes" type of space? Are we building specific parameters for the improv, whether focusing on slower scenework or applying a genre? Once we create the space, we need to allow the performers to let loose freely. We need to get out of their way.

Recently, I took on direction of Ka-Baam!!, an improvised comic book adventure show. Prior to this, I had been a member of the cast for three years under the direction of the show's creator, Steve Wacker, a talented and insightful improviser with a vast knowledge of the comics genre (in fact, he went on to be an editor at DC Comics). While I had been a fan of comic books since an early age, I had nowhere near the level of understanding of the medium that he had.

My first decision was to not approach the show the same way as Steve. He would revel in the clichés of comic books and find ways to build narratives with them. Instead, I used my experience as a performer in the previous run as my guide. It's great when the performers pull out those referential chestnuts related to a particular genre, creating an in-joke for those in the know, on top of the strong improv being done. I, however, chose to mine the collective group for what they loved about comic books instead of what they knew about them. One cast member spoke about the huge suspension of disbelief in comic book storytelling; another spoke of how he could relate to the stories that dealt with being outcasts or having troubled relationships; another was just a fan of kick-ass action stories. The result was finding an "in" for the performers to follow into the work, since they all had different levels of knowledge about comic books, a few surpassing my own. This entry into the improv started to create a common vocabulary that I could exploit in the sidecoaching.

This is an example of two different spaces being created for the improvisers based on the same show with two different directing styles that went along with them. In the first, there was a level of knowledge that needed to be maintained with the fun being in exploiting the clichés. In the latter, the space was one of varied knowledge with the fun being in exploiting personal takes on the material. Both accomplished the job the best possible way for the director in charge.

> I used to check in a lot. I'd check in and say "Does this make sense? Is everybody with me? Is this helpful to you?" And in a way it was showing my own self doubt in my communication, and I know that I've stopped doing that, or at least I do it a lot less. I check in to say maybe, "Want to do more of these?" That kind of thing, to make sure the class is at least getting something in what we're doing. In the beginning I would be much more doubtful of what we were working on and that's a huge thing to overcome just because I think if you've ever been in a class where you don't trust the teacher leading you down the path then you kind of fail, you back off on it. I didn't have too much of that, but I did know I was sending the wrong message by being doubtful.
>
> —Bob Dassie

At the beginning of any process, you want to present a set of strong ideas to build from. Some directors shy away from asserting their philosophy as the be all and end all. They swing completely the other way by not giving their cast anything to work from. This will not protect you from derision. Make a strong offer to your cast as to something that they can play with or work from. The actors will then interpret those ideas through the improvisational choices they make.

Your focus will evolve rehearsal to rehearsal from a more theoretical place to a purely observational one, showing the performers where the improv is working best, not just in the parameters of your vision, but in general. Remember, we are in an entertainment business, however fringe it is; that can be easy to lose sight of when we are too enmeshed in the process. At some point, you will need to switch out of the role of the director and into that of an audience member. You will still be able to make pointed observations of the work but hopefully you will be removed enough so as to not get in the way of it. It is possible to be too close and, in doing so, stifle the cast.

If you look back at all the teachers you've had throughout your years of education, you will notice recurring archetypes. There is the tyrannical teacher, the fatherly teacher, the cool egalitarian, the one who makes the lessons fun, the one who just reads from the textbook. As directors, we all fall into similar archetypes and it is helpful to note which you are and cultivate it.

Johnstone was keenly aware of the perceptions his new students had of him. He is considered a guru and this labelling can create a distracting distance between the teacher and student. Sitting on the floor is one of the ways he would help alter that perception so he could better direct them. I have also heard stories of him entering classrooms acting befuddled to make himself more accessible.

The persona you put across is a great tool and most people are not aware of theirs. They are making it up as they go along and it is reflected in how they carry themselves when leading. I know some directors who are intimidated by their cast because they feel the players are more talented than they or more experienced. Your observations are always valid as such and should not be discounted.

It doesn't matter how long the group you are directing or coaching has been around, or what they have done before. You are in the position you are in for a reason. There was an agreement to that before you stepped up in front of them to lead for the first time. Players can disagree with you, but they should not be allowed to disregard you. Your ideas will only go as far as you push them.

Regardless of whether you are doing a very strict lesson plan or you are creating an open workshop where you are looking to discover people's parameters, you want to give a strong sense of self. People are looking to you to lead them and you need to show them direction not only in what you say but how you say it. Body language, phrasing, eye contact, speed of speech, all of these are tools that we use when trying to play characters of different status. These tools are equally valuable to access in leading a group.

> I do, when I walk in [to the] first class, try to be friendly and accessible. I want the students to feel at ease, that they truly can do whatever they want. I know I also intentionally curse when I see the attention waning and see that they don't understand how important this thing is that I am trying to teach them, how really important it is to me and how truly important it is to performance in general. So I use the word "fuck" and it immediately gets their attention, it's very titillating. I can't believe that it's 2005 and the word "fuck" is so titillating but it is. And I feel like that's my edgy persona. I don't think it's edgy but I think that it's perceived that way. I also think it helps make me more accessible in a way too.
>
> *—Rebecca Sohn*

It is like I said about choices. It is impossible to not make one. It is the same with personae. If you are curious as to your persona, record yourself at your next rehearsal or workshop. Not the entire workshop, just from the beginning through the first couple of exercises.

When you have the recording, review it objectively. For instance, time how long between the start of the rehearsal and when everyone gets up. Look at how many times you use the words "could" or "might" as opposed to "will" and "should." See how often you use phrases with "no," "don't" or "not" in them. These factors seem small but they make a world of difference to frailer or less focused students.

> A lot of times when we find ourselves in front of the room with the "Coach" or "Teacher" hat on, we feel the need to know everything. Younger coaches and teachers usually end up talking too much to the class/team/cast for the same reason that younger improvisers end up talking too much in scenes.....fear and overcompensation, for a bunch of internal stuff...fear and overcompensation almost always show up first verbally (as opposed to behaviorally) in improv.....especially for the "authority" standing in front of the room.
>
> *—Joe Bill*

There is no one persona that trumps all others. There is no one way of leading a class that eliminates interactive issues. Being able to come across as stern when you need to be or concise when you need to be or befuddled when you need to be gives you more control of the direction of the group.

The bottom line is do not be afraid to define yourself in your philosophies and approach. Allow yourself to be wrong and adapt every once in a while. It is a stronger place to build from than from a place of vagueness so as to appeal to everyone with whom you are working.

VOICE OF THE DIRECTOR VS. VOICE OF THE TROUPE

I'm exploring with the cast in the first couple of meetings exactly what it is that I want to say and how what they want to say in the same direction influences that.

—*Don Hall*

We have a collection of improvisers. As varied as their styles or experience or frames of reference may be, there develops an overlap that is the ensemble. It is our job to recognize what makes that ensemble different from all others. What is their voice and how does it differ from that of the individuals? How does it differ from yours for that matter?

Voice is different from *group mind*, that magical connection that occurs when a group is able to finish each other's thoughts onstage. That is a metaphysical connection, and it is hoped that all groups have this to some degree. Their voice is closer to their image or style, the way that a band has a style. It is the method by which they play that umbrellas all the individual moments. The Clash is their own unique collaboration and even when they are doing a cover of someone else's songs, it is interpreted through that image. The voice is what makes the group who they are.

If we go too far into this, you are going to get lost in your head. Trust that eventually you will recognize what is special about the group that you are working with and how to foster it. Trust your observations of them and experiment with the challenges that you give them as a group. The more direct and specific the challenge, the more pronounced the response they give as they play through it.

One aspect of their work that makes up their voice is their style, which is easy to spot. There are groups that love to play blue, play broadly, play it straight, play the fantastical, etc. Another aspect of their work that gives a sense of their voice is the rhythm by which they play. When a group plays together, they tend to match each other's tempo. Some groups will hit a lot of quick scenes at the top that get longer as the show continues. Another might play one long scene with cutaways to other locations and storylines. Where as a group do they speed up? Where do they take their time?

It is not always the same for all players across the board stylistically, but it is a good place to start discussion, particularly with those players who are not in on those stylistic choices. Wild card players, those who stand out from the pack can provide nice surprises in a performance that keep the rest of the cast on their toes. If people are too familiar with each other's work, they can get complacent about jumping to completely new directions. (The idea of stand-out players is always tricky anyway when working in such a collaborative artform as improv.)

> You have to look at not only individual energy that people bring and the things that they bring to the table but also sort of like the group hierarchy. People will automatically start deferring certain things to each other. And that's always an interesting concept: how to use that as strength but not let it become a crutch of the group.
>
> —*Mark Sutton*

Finally, if we are following the ball, how does this apply with the group as a whole? Do they follow plot points into the next scene? Characters? Do they jump on thematic tangents? Do the scenes seem unrelated to each other at all? Possibly, the group has not yet come to an agreement as to what the overall arc is of the show. Maybe they need to or they might be better off without it. There are no surefire answers that I can give here, only places to look.

As you develop as a director, you too will find yourself gravitating toward certain ideas and applying those to all projects of which you are a part. There is a trickiness, however, to creating your cohesive vision for a show while still allowing the performers the freedom to make individual choices.

> If you're fighting too hard to make something happen and it just keeps on failing, chances are it's not something organic. When you direct improv you're part of "Yes And" too. You've got to realize that. Some directors will try to make people do something that's just not natural, it's just not organic and the cast will get frustrated because it just never works and it doesn't matter how much you prod people into it.
>
> —*Armando Diaz*

As you go through your rehearsals, your job will be to hold tightly to the philosophy while letting go of the details. The format is not the star and anything specific to it is malleable. That fabulous editing technique or bold vocabulary of choices that you have introduced are not so precious that they cannot be excised for the betterment of the show. The philosophy of your work exists in how choices are made and not in what choices are made.

Look at the desired quality of the show: fast and furious, slowly building, highly irreverent. Each of these concepts can be played infinite ways. Let the cast surprise you in the choices that are made and help point them toward those choices rather than point them out.

When coaching, the troupe's voice overrides yours. The group that you are coming to work with will have a sensibility, hopefully, that is particular to them. Once again, we are not talking about the format but the way in which they attack the scenework or whatever building blocks are inherent to their performances (e.g., monologues, soundscapes, etc.).

AUDITIONING MEMBERS

> Casting is the hardest part of directing improv, I think, because once you do that and you have a good cast, you can relax enough to know that whatever situation they get themselves into...they're good enough to get themselves out.
>
> —*Dan O'Connor*

People have often asked me how they should run auditions for their troupe, as if there is only one way. The audition process is a reflection of the group's work to all those who try out. How you as director organize the audition shows what is most important to you artistically, while giving the actors the chance to show their best. So what do you look for most in an improviser? What skills can they simply not be without? What skills are you willing to overlook a lack in? This speaks specifically to what you feel you can pull out of a performer easily and what you can't.

> As a director, the last thing I want to do is teach someone. That's not what I am there for when I'm directing. I'm there to help them shape a show. If they're not ready to make that show, then maybe they shouldn't be part of that process.
>
> —*Kevin Mullaney*

For example—and this is specific to me—I look for strong initiative in any player. While I have challenges and exercises that can help deal with hesitancy in players, I find it difficult to make the change stick. Possible, but difficult. So, for the sake of initiative I am willing to compromise on other aspects like variety of character. That speaks to what I can direct.

Another big consideration is dynamic, and this depends on the project you are filling slots for. Troupes with ongoing rehearsals and shows will want as varied a cast as possible. You might want a mix of players who do fast and furious as well as those that can do longer, slower scenework. You might want players who are good at playing real as well as ones who are good at playing outrageous characters. Varying up the rhythms of a troupe helps cover all bases for any show and exposes current members to new ways of playing. If you are auditioning for a specific project, then what you need has already been decided. A genre-heavy show would be most benefited by players with a working knowledge of that genre and the ability to play different archetypes easily. A troupe that does children's shows would want someone who plays big with their physicality and voice.

Now that you know what you're looking for, you can structure your auditions accordingly. Traits can be divided into two categories: individual or group. If your auditions will be focused more on the individual, rapid-fire monologues done in succession or any similar quick glimpses might display their talents more than drawn-out scenes. Group characteristics, on the other hand, such as teamwork and editing can be better displayed mixing as often as possible. That calls for looser scheduling of longer audition slots with several auditioners at a time. Think about the environment that will best showcase what you want to see. Because I am looking for strong initiative, I know that I will set up half-hour slots where I can see five to six people at a time. The audition will be composed mostly of short scenes to give people plenty of chances to enter.

Improv auditions are awkward for the actors who are trying out. They are supposed to work together with the people they are competing against. This conflict creates questions for the improvisers such as how much to hold back and whether or not to do walk-ons. Prepare the actors with a focus, explaining to them specifically what you are looking for. Letting them know what the goal is helps keep them focused on the scene rather than on each other. Albeit, there is a temptation to see if the actors will deliver the goods on their own, to try to find the genius who knows exactly what to do without your needing to prompt them. That means less work for you, right? Perhaps, but ultimately, there is considerably more satisfaction in finding those people who are directable. Give the players the challenge and see who satisfies it. If you convey that your project requires playing lots of different characters but the actors continue to play very closely to themselves, then your job is made considerably easier in weeding out those who need too much work.

Some directors might want to create two levels of priorities, saving the second for callbacks where you look at a narrowed-down list of auditionees. This gives the opportunity to focus on the individual in the first round and the group dynamics at the callbacks.

Who should you have with you at the audition? Regardless of whether you are the sole director of the troupe or not, second opinions can be incredibly helpful, especially from those who will be playing side by side with the new recruits. Use your troupe to the benefit of the audition process whether it be getting auditioners warmed up prior to their slot, taking notes at the auditions, or mixing them into the scenework to gain a perspective of which improvisers are most fun to play with. Once again, this depends on how you structure your audition and on what skill you value most.

Make sure you are clear with all other attending representatives of the troupe on the image that you want put across. This means having a very focused image that comes across in any distributed handouts, on the voice mail where people call to confirm and at the desk where they are first greeted.

In the audition room, create space where attending troupe members can voice their opinions and concerns in a way that does not conflict with your presentation as director. This can be by creating a few minutes of review between audition slots or by officially opening the floor to questions and comments from the troupe during the audition. Even if your group has a shared directorship, make sure to have a single figurehead to present to auditioners, feeling free to rotate the positions from slot to slot, in order to keep the event running smoothly.

CHAPTER 5: STRUCTURING REHEARSALS AND WORKSHOPS

> Be willing to bend, because as soon as you hit your vision, and as soon as things come together, it will open up new possibilities. Be able to embrace all of those things.
>
> —*Bob Dassie*

My friend Matt Dominianni once explained to me how an individual's collective knowledge could be divided into three areas: what we know that we know, what we know that we don't know, and what we don't know that we don't know. One of the biggest pitfalls for directors is when they confine their thinking too much to one of these areas.

Directors overcome by what they know that they know can have trouble adapting to the needs of their cast and can be blind to the surprising gifts that come from the varied interpretations of their instructions. Directors overcome by what they know that they don't know have trouble leading. Status is a necessary and fragile tool for an instructor, which is greatly diminished by too much uncertainty. Finally, directors overcome by what they don't know that they don't know become overly ethereal and abstract about the work, avoiding the concrete observations which help the cast recreate good work in the future. A rehearsal needs to be the best possible balance between education, exploration and discipline.

The director needs to be the best improviser in the room—not as a performer, but as an acute observer of all that is going on. Balancing time constraints with a meaty lesson plan while keeping survey over the players' personal problems versus what the group as a whole needs to work on is an incredibly daunting task. There is a chance that you will fail the first time you attempt the position. It will get easier each time you return, I promise.

EDUCATION VERSUS EXPLORATION

Rehearsals can follow different tracks based on that day's purpose; some are educational sessions while others are strictly exploratory. Educational sessions are focused on developing the individuals and adding to their toolbox of skills. This in no way denotes the skill level of the troupe—that they are clueless on the topic and need to be taught the basics. For instance, perhaps you have decided to devote an entire rehearsal to character. You want to see people create many different personality types or play characters that are as far from the personality of the players as possible. The session is structured with a strong idea of an end result in mind, with exercises and games that can be used to reach that goal.

Exploratory sessions are focused on developing a concept through experimentation with the troupe, such as the creation of a new format or discovering how to communicate new edits. Exploration begins with a set of strong ideas to build from, and can develop in any unknown direction. For example, I once led a couple of workshops to develop Somedance, an improvisation based on the storytelling styles of independent films. I knew there were certain editing techniques and archetypes that I wanted to play with but had no idea on how that would translate into improvisational choices. The theories needed to be put into action to be developed further, so I pulled together some actors that I knew to workshop it. We watched some scenes from movies and mimicked them so as to see what choices people made to parallel the director's choices in the movies (which we discuss later in Working From Templates).

Distinguishing between the educational rehearsal and the exploratory rehearsal is helpful in structuring your attack plan (which is similar to a lesson plan, although it is also applicable to a rehearsal). It creates a mission statement for each day's work which makes all the other decisions easier:

1. *What kind of environment do we need to establish?* By letting my players know that the session is an exploration, we can eliminate the pressure of "mistakes" being made. You will be on a more equal level with the rest of the group, which brings with it a more playful atmosphere. Educational sessions are more of a "this is what I want to see" type of experience.

2. *How do I structure the rehearsal?* Educational sessions tend to follow a "discussion and application" approach. First, components of the topic are workshopped through pertinent exercises. Perhaps handouts are distributed—such as when you are rehearsing a

certain genre and wish to pull directly from a playwright's work. The exercises tend to be more structured to point toward the desired result, such as in the way that playing Status Switch will have the actors experiencing both sides of a status relationship in a given scene. Exploratory rehearsals are more freeform. With Somedance, we used the scenes from specific movies as templates, not as a way to point the actors toward a result, but to learn how they got to the result that developed. For instance, it was not as important to get the cast to do montages as to see how they would communicate the initiation of a montage with each other. Each new discovery would inform the next stretch of the rehearsal.

3. *How should the rehearsal flow from moment to moment?* If you are exploring a new idea, you may never need to see a full scene, opting instead to run a quick succession of scene openings. You may also not feel the need to run all the actors through each exercise, opting instead to move on to another idea. If you are running an educational rehearsal, you might require all the actors to play each exercise so that they see how it feels to play within that game's set of rules. Improv is best learned when it is hands-on.

4. *What will we have at the end?* Educational rehearsals are for adding a technique to the improviser's toolbox; for example, if the goal is to have them internalize a particular way to initiate scenes or develop characters that they can take with them into any show. Exploratory rehearsals may not be as tangible. At the end, the actors may come away with something for the toolbox but it may be only partially developed. The end result is left to chance in the same way all improvised scenes are when they begin.

In the case of an exploration, I am willing to let go of notes on individual performance. Of course, Somedance was made easier by my workshop having been invite-only. Knowing the performers and their skills beforehand allowed me to put my focus on the development of the concept. Regardless, when working with any troupe of actors you need to prioritize your notes more than ever so as to develop the idea. Once that is set, you can adapt the players as need be in their individual approaches to the improvisation. As we discussed earlier, improv is made up of choices and commitment. If we are not sure yet as to what kind of choices we are looking for, all other observations are moot.

THE OPENING SPIEL

> The first, most grievous sin when you are working in improvisation or text or whatever, is to walk in and feel so intimidated by the situation or by the people or by feeling like your butt's on the line, or getting your ego in the way, that you walk in and try to micromanage and over-control the situation, which is going to make your cast want to kick your ass and get you out of the situation within about 10-12 days. You're done. The second most grievous sin, I think, of a beginning director is to under-control—to be so wishy-washy in [your] vision of the world and of [yourselves] and of the work that should be on the stage, they're unable to give feedback to the cast, to give notes or to give ideas, to be part of the process.
>
> —*Michael Gellman*

Just as you might practice the opening of a show, you should rehearse the opening spiel of the session. This is where you address generally what will be covered and any other pertinent information.

Here is the spiel that I use when teaching a two-hour Directing Improv class at a festival, which I have labelled for analysis below:

> (a) Hello, everyone. My name is Asaf Ronen and I will be leading the next two hours of your life. I have been doing improv since 1990: Theatresports, ComedySportz, Harolds, freeform structures, improvised two-act plays, improvised musicals, and several original longform structures that I have helped create. I have been teaching and directing improv since 1997. I have worked with all levels, from Kindergarten students up to adult improvisers like yourselves. (b) I have very specific philosophies and techniques that have helped me along the way which I am going to share with you. Today, we will look at giving notes, sidecoaching and general rehearsal maintenance. (c) In the last twenty minutes, I will open the class up to a Q&A so we can address any directing- or improv-related questions that you might still have.

This entire spiel takes under two minutes because I have practiced it and trimmed it down where necessary. If you are taking longer than that, you may be sharing information that can be saved for later in the session. What the class needs to know varies from situation to situation, but there are categories you should hit that follow a past-present-future structure.

a) *Background.* This is helpful with new groups that you are working with or when teaching, particularly when working out of town. It gives people a way to relate to you and allows you to assert status if you feel that is necessary. In teaching a directing improv class, for example, I feel obligated to mention not just the breadth of my work but the variety of forms that I have worked in as a way to let people know that the techniques I am showing them can be applied to whatever type of work they are doing. If you are rehearsing on an ongoing basis with a troupe, the background will most likely be restricted to what was worked on last week to refresh it in people's minds and to create a strong foundation for that day's lesson.

b) *The Plan.* This is where we briefly discuss what the focus of the day is. The key word is briefly. My spiel is nothing more than a quick three-point list. Some directors get too involved at the top as to what specific exercises will be done or what end results will be achieved. These are often repeated later on in the session anyway and don't require an early mention.

c) *Safeguarding for later.* Saying that there will be a Q&A at the end of the session usually reduces the questions to only the most important. Similarly, mentioning when the break will be will limit interruptions from people needing to go to the bathroom or to make a call. People can hold out for such things as long as they know how long they will be holding for.

Remember, the opening spiel sets the tone for the session. It gives the actors a sense of how to relate to you and to the rehearsal that lays before them. As such, the opening warrants a significant amount of your attention to make sure that it achieves its maximum potential.

DELEGATION

Just because you are the director doesn't mean that you need to do it all yourself. Delegating segments of a rehearsal can create a stronger working environment in a number of ways:

- It shares responsibility among all the members. This keeps your performers more invested in the troupe.

- It frees you up to take a more objective look at the work. Keeping a rehearsal running divides your attention and it is helpful to your primary goal of building an ensemble to have moments of narrower focus.

- It benefits you to have followers who can also step into the role of leader. This will develop certain improv skills which require a director's eye, such as editing. You will also benefit from having someone who can properly direct you when you choose to perform.

The easiest and best place to delegate is when warming up. Warm-ups are for the performers' benefit anyway, so allowing the players to lead them better guarantees that they are in fact warmed up. Survey your group and you will find others with leadership experience who can also lead specific exercises. Once you develop the vocabulary for your troupe you can easily hand the reins over for brief stints and regain the control when necessary. This allows you to watch from a distance when you need to get a good overview of the troupe without being distracted, or to make adjustments in your attack plan.

I make sure to have a catalog of quick exercises that I can follow anything up with. This helps me regain focus, and thus control, of the rehearsal. Even a simple moment of the group inhaling and exhaling under your leadership helps put you back in the seat of authority.

LANGUAGE FOR EXERCISES & INTRODUCTIONS

We should always assume that an exercise needs explanation when we are working with new people, regardless of how experienced they are. As we discussed in *Breaking Down the Work*, there is an improv shorthand for everything, yet we take our own meanings for granted. There are dozens of variations of so many games and exercises that go by the same name and dozens of names that refer to the same exercises. It is worth the effort to provide a setup that eliminates any possible confusion.

The most important thing to mention is what the focus is of any warm-up. This is also taken for granted. Even as simple an exercise as Zip Zap Zop can be done for different reasons. For those who do not know the exercise, it's where everyone gets in a circle to pass energy. They do so by clapping at someone in the circle and yelling "Zip." That person claps at someone and yells "Zap" who then claps at someone and yells "Zop." This goes on and on across the circle, saying those three words in increasingly quick succession as the energy is passed around. Fairly simple.

Somehow, however, people still hesitate in this game. I have seen people pause because they weren't sure who to pass it to or because they screwed up the order of words. If there are pauses or confusion of any kind, then most likely the focus is not clear. Are we playing Zip Zap Zop to develop group awareness (in which case we might have several running simultaneously), mental acuity (in which case we might play the variation where any rhyming triplet can be initiated such as Nip Nap Nop or Bip Bap Bop), or are we just focusing on building momentum which strengthens the idea that it really does not matter who we pass to and what word we use? As I said, take nothing for granted.

Also, trust that there will be chances to explore further along the way, rather than set several challenges at once. Let's say we are doing a physical exercise like Complementary Sculptures (listed in the Appendix) where the players are jumping into poses that relate to each other. Giving a focus of making really dynamic poses that also engage the face and making sure that the players also explore distance from each other and are using different levels is too much for them to take in at the top. Instead, sidecoach them as the exercise progresses. Let them get comfortable with the one angle, dynamic poses, and introduce new challenges along the way to grow their physical toolbox.

CREATING A CATALOG OF EXERCISES

Exercises are meant to be unique to the group of people using them. As you develop yourself as a director, you will, more and more, develop your own exercises to tend to the specific needs of your cast and to help explore your own improvisational ideas.

As we saw in the chapter on notes, any pattern can be taken on with the right challenge. Similarly, any challenge can be made into an exercise. Challenges need not be person-specific as much as they are directions into new tools that any player can learn from taking on themselves. In Appendix B of this book, I have listed some exercises that have been created by me or introduced to me by colleagues through the years. Doing exercises from a book can be tricky because they are open to interpretation and can thus change their intent. If there is an exercise described that you don't fully understand but still feel the need to try, I invite you to misinterpret it. Ultimately, the intent of the exercise is secondary to the change it produces in the players who attempt it. A change will always happen by virtue of the fact that you are doing something new. Whatever the result, consider it your personal variation on the exercise.

> Don't shy away from a rehearsal which is ritualistic...If you find exercises that you like, that seem fruitful, do them a lot. Don't be afraid to do the same rehearsal over again.
>
> —*Kevin Mullaney*

I know there is a joy to doing a new exercise, particularly for the director who introduces it to the others. That is the attitude that makes improv a perfect fit for us. It can feel powerful and spiritual to share a new discovery. But if you're focused on strengthening your ensemble, then you will want to share a solid frame of reference. The exercises the troupe does together and the skills that they develop during them are a huge part of that. If an exercise is only tried at one or two rehearsals, then there is a chance that the players will come away with their own varied interpretations.

> People put too much pressure on themselves to bring in new exercises every time. And then, when they run out of those exercises, after six weeks or nine weeks or fifteen weeks, they're sort of spent as a coach...A basketball coach doesn't bring in new exercises every week. He has a set of exercises or set of things they do in practice and you do those things over and over again. To practice, to get better, to learn things through the process of doing.
>
> —*Kevin Mullaney*

If you find the troupe plateauing, not developing any further in a certain exercise, that is the best time to shake things up with something new. You can also create variations on any exercise you are currently using to get a fresh perspective. Play with the tempo or the scope, put a twist on one of the rules (the chapter on Creating Formats will elaborate on directions for this). New ideas can always be squeezed out of even the oldest games.

Don't let boredom solely dictate when you bring in new things to play with. Even deadlier is when an exercise is retired because it is hard. The only way to get better at something is by doing it again and again. Avoiding difficult challenges means missing out on perfect opportunities for improvisers to push their limits.

PHYSICALIZING YOUR SHORTHAND

Whenever I teach a class or lead a rehearsal there are four things that I always make sure to have on hand, just in case I need them: a notebook, a timer, a bell captain's bell, and a roll of masking tape. The purpose of the notebook is obvious. The other objects are there to set parameters on the scenes for particular exercises.

The length of a scene is the most recognizable parameter to play with. Players play differently when they know they only have thirty seconds left on the clock and even more differently when the clock only starts with thirty seconds. Timers are also helpful in keeping track of certain performers' rhythms. In one class I taught, there was an actor who would start off all his scenes slowly until thirty to forty-five seconds in, when he would react suddenly to something and make the scene about that. As we discussed in the chapter on giving notes, there is nothing inherently wrong with playing this way, but it helps to try different rhythms. What if he were to start a few scenes in a row with a big reaction right away? What if he were to pack as many emotions as possible into one scene?

The bell is one way that I have of creating a shorthand for my directions. For example, if I am directing a scene where I want the improvisers to explore the environment more, then I would tell them that every time I ring the bell they need to grab an imagined object from space. The bell tends to be a cleaner way to cue actors than doing it vocally. There have been many times when they could not hear the direction over the dialogue of the scene, causing them to stop and ask me what I said. By setting the meaning beforehand, such as by saying that every time I ring it the scene must continue in silence (thus making it easier to make wordier sidecoaches), I find I can coach more efficiently.

The tape can serve a number of different purposes when applied to the surfaces of the rehearsal space. It can help create a stage of a certain size or shape when training to perform at a particular venue. Sight points can be created by placing Xs on the wall when you need to focus an actor's gaze during a monologue or while playing MC. If scenes are starting very similarly in their energy, I can lay down lines that actors must follow into the scene. Or I can lay down marks for them to hit. There is also the option to create certain designations on the stage. When I want to see more monologues in the scenework, I draw out a box where they can happen, providing a constant reminder of that option. Not only will there be more monologues but the choice to do so will become more pronounced. The players will begin to recognize when someone is about to do a monologue before they step into the box, and when they are wrapping it up before they step out. (I recommend using painter's masking tape as it comes off surfaces most easily and the colors it is available in stand out best in any space.)

WORKING FROM TEMPLATES

In exploring new forms, formats or concepts, it is a good idea to have a template for the performers to work from. Viola Spolin understood this best of all. The games that she provides in *Improvisation for Theater* are templates that allow children easier access to the principles of improv.

In the case of Somedance, I wanted to experiment with different editing techniques based on what I was seeing done in independent films. That genre, inherent to working outside the studio system, was ripe with new ideas on how to play out a narrative. I decided that the best way to start was to review some scenes from movies and use them as templates, to perform improvised parallels of the scenes. With Somedance, we looked at scenes from specific movies and used them as templates—not as a way to point the actors toward a result, but to learn how they got to the result that developed. For instance, how would they communicate the initiation of a montage? Each new discovery would inform the next stretch of the rehearsal.

One clip we used was a time jump montage from John Sayles' *Passion Fish*. In the movie, Mary McDonnell plays an aging soap opera star who has been incapacitated by an accident. She becomes bitter, not only because she can't work but because she has to rely upon the aid of an in-home nurse. The montage comes early on in the movie as McDonnell goes through several nurses who for one reason or another do not work out. Sayles has some particular nuances in this sequence. The editing is always done on a movement, either of the camera, or of a person moving across the frame. Also, with each new segment in the montage, McDonnell's character takes up less space while saying fewer words, eventually doing nothing more than grunting back at the nurse. Finally, the lighting gets darker and darker until we are introduced to Alfre Woodard's character as she gets off a bus in bright, bright daylight, dressed in a nurse's uniform. The edit is sudden in the lighting jump, signifying that Woodard is the nurse who is going to stay.

After viewing the scene, I challenged the performers to improvise that same scene structure using different scenarios (a string of bad dates, a series of short-lived jobs) with the focus on communicating the edit into each new scene of the montage as well as communicating the change in scene that will end the montage (like the Alfre Woodard scene). Once that concept is grasped we can start to pull away from the template. Without the scenario in place, how easy is it for the actors to find the throughline for a montage? How easy is it for them to communicate the edit into the montage? How easy is it for the players to communicate the end of a montage similarly to Woodard's appearance in the clip? After that it is a matter of fitting it into a longer improvised piece and seeing how well they read each other's editing initiations. A vocabulary of initiation has now been created as well as building techniques that are easily recognized by any member of the group. From there we can move onto more complicated templates—the Holy Grail of which is The Commode Story scene from *Reservoir Dogs*.

PLANNING A REHEARSAL SCHEDULE

> It's not the kind of thing where you can just tell people their ideas, tell people "just do this." You have to bring them there, you have to bring them there a step at a time. You have to give them the experiences that they would have in the show and have them find it in small parts.
>
> —*Armando Diaz*

In planning out a rehearsal schedule for a specific format, it is helpful to work backwards through the process to ensure enough time is devoted to each step. The steps that I look at, in reverse order, are as follows: Tech Rehearsal, Run-Through, Dress Rehearsal, Dry Run, Components, Stylistic Scenes, Skill Set Rehearsals, General Mix-Up. Each of these steps can range in depth from a fraction of a rehearsal to several consecutive rehearsals, sometimes overlapping. The following explains what is accomplished in each of the steps, assuming a unique format or variation of a known format. Freeform and shortform improv projects will not need some of the steps listed.

General Mix-Up. When bringing improvisers together for the first time, it is best to focus on the joy of improvisation and not impose the needs of the show upon the group—yet. The ensemble will need to develop a rhythm with each other before that rhythm can be molded to the project. This will also give you a chance to observe the individual performers' patterns and which interpersonal dynamics are strongest. If your show requires casting people in specific roles, you will find yourself better-informed by giving yourself the purest view of their work possible.

Skill Set Rehearsals. This is where we start to apply that which is the key aspect of the show to the rehearsal process. If the show is focused on character, this is where we would run the ensemble through character-building exercises. How long you run skill-set rehearsals depends on how many key skill sets you need to work on and how extensive the show's take on that skill needs to be. It is assumed that the troupe already possesses adequate skills. In initiating skill set rehearsals we are exploring a new approach to—or take on—that skill. It is possible that this can be done in one rehearsal, depending on your show.

Stylistic Scenes. This is building the skill set into scenes, games and monologues, applying the new take. This is most prevalent in shows influenced or modeled after specific genres. A troupe improvising Shakespearean plays might explore the skill of verbal imagery and metaphor in their dialogue and use this stage to expand that in two-person dialogues (what is known as a conceit). A Commedia-based show would use the skill set rehearsals to develop specific characters by exploring how they interact with each other.

Components. Many formats have markers and editing techniques that are specific to their show. A musical improv show is a good example, as a thorough troupe would want to explore solo songs, group songs with passed verses, and duets. The Shakepearean troupe would investigate improvising soliloquys and how to best initiate that from within the scene. This also includes Harold teams that are crafting a unique opening game.

Dry Run. Once you have covered the individual components and stylistic touches, you would put them together into one cohesive piece, giving yourself room to tweak or even eliminate certain ideas. This will be fully explored in *Creating Formats with Your Troupe*. A dry run can involve a lot of stopping and starting of the piece to better address the issues of cohesion.

Dress Rehearsal. Some formats involve high production values, namely props, costumes and set pieces. You want to give yourself a chance to discover the surprises inherent in incorporating these elements into the show. A costume piece may hinder movement in a way that you did not consider, or the performers' choices are limited by having to fetch certain props before initiating them. If you use a musician in your show this is the latest time at which you would want to bring them into the process.

Run-Through. Unlike the dry run, this is a straight run of the show without interruption. You want to see how your performers are able to maintain their choices and what sort of problems occur along the way. Remember, the actors' main tools are their instincts and you want to see how those work when there is no safety net to better prepare them for performance conditions.

Tech Rehearsal. This is where you adjust for space and lighting. From where will the actors enter? Where will that special solo spotlight be? What will the lighting look like when initiating a transition between scenes? Most tech rehearsals rarely include a full run-through of the show, if any improv at all, so make sure all issues are resolved prior to this point.

DISCUSSIONS DURING REHEARSAL

It's fine to be open to a dialogue, but a director also has to know when to shut that dialogue up and get working because its much safer to talk about things than to do them.

—*Mark Sutton*

Opening up discussions is a necessary tool but it presents a hazard to watch for—the slipping of power, and thus of focus. Discussions about the work can happen, as long as they happen on your terms. There is a fine line between a healthy question-and-answer interchange to help a player get a better understanding, and the overindulgence of a player who is explaining what they "intended" in a particular choice. The former is a part of their self-growth, the latter is an act of self-protection and the line between them gets crossed too often.

The biggest risk to progress is when discussions begin right before a new exercise or idea is explored. The amount of dialogue a player may initiate as a means of safeguarding himself under the guise of trying to better understand, can be staggering. The best way to understand any improv theory is through practice, not discussion. If the focus or parameters of an exercise have been explained satisfactorily enough for you but there is a player who needs further explanation, push forward and give that player permission to misunderstand. This is where a director needs to step up and say, "While those are wonderful and inspired ideas, let's try it this way first and *then* modify it as needed."

Maybe they won't hit the mark themselves, but they will see others around them illustrating what you are talking about. Perhaps, they will even reinvent the exercise by misinterpreting it—a golden opportunity.

> When all the explanations are done I get people up and try to get them to have the experience of it, because the experience of it is what stays with you, not the words.
>
> —Bob Dassie

Some directors go completely the opposite way, overdiscussing ideas, in their own attempt at self-protection. Learn to be comfortable without discussion, particularly if you have nothing to add. Your job is to give the rehearsal process cohesion, not a play-by-play. It is perfectly alright to let a string of scenes go by without interjecting a word. Let the teacher in you find what needs to be said, rather than the ego that wants to make sure it is relevant.

GIVING HOMEWORK

As we discussed in the notes chapter, you can give people your observations but ultimately it is up to them to change. You have no power over them. A companion rule to this is that you can give your troupe homework but there is no guarantee that they will do it. They are not horrible people and it is not that they aren't serious about the work. Some may even come to you soliciting an assignment (in which case you might want to toy with the idea of a syllabus, just in case). The point is to not hinge the progress of the rehearsal on whether or not the homework was done. Homework needs to be its own reward, otherwise not only will it not be done, it will be regarded derisively.

> Anything that's essential should be done as a group, i.e, sit down and watch key scenes and talk about them together because you can't trust people to do it thoughtfully if they do it alone.
>
> —Jill Bernard

Instead, create homework that will enhance the lessons. That way, if it isn't done, the rehearsal isn't impeded. Anyone who has done their assignment will have a deeper understanding at the next session. The best format for these assignments is as a syllabus. Let's suppose that you are working on a new format with a set narrative structure. A suggestion of books or movies that further illustrate the concept would be helpful for those who have the time and motivation. Those who have neither will not fall behind and may be more enthused to commit the time as more and more of their teammates go through the process. The best syllabus lists a good mix of media. Some people prefer to get their information from books, others prefer a visual medium like movies. This also allows for people to find the tasks that will better fit their schedule.

Another option is the take-home exercises, either solo improvisations that the performer can do in front of the mirror or interactive games that they can try in everyday life (e.g., "do your shopping in character"). There is no way to monitor the effects of these exercises or any simple way to discuss the effect during rehearsal time, especially if it turns out that half the troupe has not tried it. But they are worth a shot with a performer who needs to explore the work in their spare time to catch up with the rest of the group. I have been in groups that have tried written homework, writing a fiction piece in a genre related to the show. While easier to monitor, I have seen this fail as well.

Remember, there are plenty of projects that succeed without issuing a single homework assignment, so don't assume that it is mandatory for progress or you will be stubbornly holding the group back yourself.

THE WRAP-UP

At the end of an educational session, reiterate what new tools have been introduced. Use specific examples from the rehearsal to help solidify the lesson. "Our first round of monologues had really strong characters and as a result they all had strong opening lines that gave us a sense of who they were." Take notice of any improvisers who were having trouble with certain exercises or falling into a recurring pattern. This shows where they were stepping out of their comfort zones and what areas they could be pushed into to explore more. Each player has an arc of how they are progressing artistically.

At the end of an exploratory session, you need to define concretely where you are in the process. Exploration can run over several rehearsals and without clear markers along the way, particularly at the end of a session, it is hard to pick up the thread again. Make a note with the troupe of any specific discoveries or decisions that came up in rehearsal. These are clear examples of when the concept worked best. "When you stepped downstage and altered your voice in the first scene, you made it very clear to the other players that you were initiating a flashback based on what your scene partner said." You now have mini-templates that can be experimented with further and expanded upon. Eventually, you want to stray from these templates and hold on to what techniques make them work. Was the flashback better communicated with a gradual transition or an immediate one? Did it help him to make eye contact with his scene partner or cut it off suddenly? Did she effectively show her character aging by melting into a new position or doing it in very distinct stages? These are questions that could come up in an exploratory session.

Rehearsals should end the same way that a note session after a show does—with an idea of what worked well and what needs to be worked on further in future sessions. The troupe should walk away from rehearsal with a strong sense of what has been accomplished and not dwell on any mistakes that they feel they made.

> There really should be no time crunch. The show should open when it's ready. I do believe that deadlines are great motivators but set them far enough in the future that you have time to rehearse properly. Don't be afraid to push back the opening if the show isn't ready. I also prefer that folks only work with one group or on one show at a time, rehearsal through performance. People tend to multi-commit. It waters down the project and causes scheduling nightmares.
>
> —*Todd Stashwick*

CHAPTER 6: SIDECOACHING

> Getting [a student] to reap the rewards of his own actions is the best way for me to get someone to buy into it, or to get them over the hump, because then they have a tangible thing and I can go, "Remember when you did that? That was good about that scene that was what helped you, remember that." And it's not necessarily the action, it's the behavior, the reaction or something that they did in that moment that will help them get over whatever hump they happen to be on.
>
> —*Bob Dassie*

If we agree that improv is created by making choices and committing to them, then we must next acknowledge that it is impossible to *not* make a choice. When the actor steps on stage she has made a choice. Granted, you hope for your players to bring more to the scene, but we are not talking about strong choices. We are talking about how all things, regardless of how subtle or bland, are choices, and that when we commit to them they become strong choices.

While giving challenges can focus specifically on choices made by the improvisers, when choices become the focus of a director's sidecoaching, it can become detrimental to the work. The art of the sidecoach is in trying to guide the player without killing the momentum of the scene in the process. The dynamic further deteriorates when the director imposes his own scene choices on the players rather than acknowledge the choices the player is already making.

Finding the choices that are being made and catching them when they are dropped is the key to helpful sidecoaching. To exercise this skill, I use the Extend/Continue game that I learned from Adam Felber while working with him in NY Theatresports, but which can be originally attributed to Keith Johnstone as Advance/Extend. Adam used the Extend/Continue exercise as a way to generate lazzi, the scripted physical or verbal routines that commedia actors would break into in the middle of their improvised storyline.

The exercise works as follows (with some slight modifications from me): one actor gets on stage to perform a silent scene involving a suggested chore. The improviser can make natural sounds (*i.e.,* sounds that people naturally make such as a laugh, a sigh, sucking through their teeth, etc.) but should shy away from making sound effects. As the player performs the activity—let's say the suggestion is painting a wall—the director calls for an aspect of that scene to be extended. Extending means that the player is focused on that aspect above all else that is occurring in the scene. For example, let's say that while painting the wall the character gets some paint on her hand that she tries to wipe off. If the director calls to "extend the wiping," the actor must focus fully on that rather than continue with the activity. This could mean becoming more anal retentive about the spots on their hand (think Lady Macbeth). Maybe the player keeps going through a cycle of cleaning her hand only to have it immediately painted on again (think Chaplin). Or the player may choose to extend the frenetic movement that comes with wiping her hand, or to heighten the frustration of never getting it clean enough, or maybe what she uses to clean her hand gets more ridiculous (e.g., water, turpentine, a belt sander). The key is that the director sees something in the scene—a choice the player has already made no matter how slight—and calls it, leaving the improviser to interpret the extension any way she can imagine. The player then keeps taking the extension further and further until the director calls to continue, at which point the actor goes back to completing the chore. The player should fade back into the task so as to not pretend that moment never happened. Whatever came up in that moment will usually carry over into the rest of the scene as a character trait, be it anal retentiveness or incompetence or flamboyance—whatever the actor latched onto.

This aspect can be representative of any of the choices that are made in the average scene. By calling these extensions, we call attention to all these choices, regardless of how small or unintentional (a.k.a. the blind offer). This is one facet of sidecoaching.

It is important for the director to keep on the improviser, to reinforce the extension that is called. Most people will jump to the Continue sooner than wanted, being convinced that what they are doing isn't "interesting enough." The truth is quite the contrary. The more focused the players, the more interested an audience will be. The director should repeat the extension until it is time to continue. This will keep the focus present for the improviser while also keeping them from plateauing in the scene.

When a player is stuck on how to take an extension further (and believe me, it can always go further) they hit a point where they are just repeating themselves without building—a plateau. This also happens in speaking scenes where the players find themselves talking aimlessly while waiting for "something to happen." In our example, it is not enough for the player to simply keep wiping her hand. There has to be a growth in emotion or circumstances that leads you to the next stage of the story or game. Optimally, this will lead you to the moment to continue. If the performer is stuck as to what to do, one of two addendum can be added to the call. Firstly, get the player to vocalize. Many improvisers tend to rely a lot on verbalization and when that is taken away they sacrifice all vocalization with it. A heavy sigh or laugh can help take an extended emotion to a whole new level. Another tactic is to prompt the player to reach immediately for an object, though some players are thrown by this request. They can get in their head about what object to create spontaneously when they are not grounded enough in the scene. For others it becomes a huge, unusual gift. If the person who is unsuccessfully wiping her hand suddenly reaches for an object that turns out to be a belt sander, she has now taken the scene to a new level. In short, this ability to suddenly reach for an object that will further the scene is a valuable skill for all improvisers to have, but not all players will succeed right away.

Huge new choices will come up in the course of playing out an extension. There will be a tendency to call attention to these choices as new extensions, like the freneticism of the movement in our previous example, or the emotion that comes out while extending the wiping. We have to keep the player focused on the main extension rather than call attention to these things to prevent narrowing down the scope. Remember, these new choices are consequences of our original call and will evolve on their own (and surprising new choices will develop) as a result of keeping on the original call. When we have more than one extension piled on top of the other, it can take a player off track and make it harder to return to the grounding of the scene or, in the case of this exercise, where they left off in the chore.

If you are having trouble reading your improvisers to the point where you cannot find an extension to call, chances are that the actor is making choices (remember, it is impossible to not make one) but is not letting it be as pronounced as it could be. Just as players censor themselves from doing something "uninteresting" for too long, they keep themselves from playing "too big." As a director, encourage them to do this in rehearsals and then scale it down as you go, if needed. If you have no reading at the top of the scene, call a general extension on emotion. Whatever emotion they thought they were conveying will now be more evident. The same can be done with physicality or attitude toward the other character or the setting of the scene.

Extend/Continue demonstrates how sidecoaching can be used for any scene. We aren't making specific choices for the players when we feel like "nothing's happening." Instead, we are pointing out the choices that they are making so that they can take them further.

This exercise is also a great tool for developing characters based on the quirks that come up through the extensions. It helps players who wish to be more physical on stage, as well as streamlining narrative. The exercise additionally can help train your musical and technical improvisers to define the beats and buttons of the scene (which will be covered in a later chapter).

The next level is the two-person Extend/Continue exercise, also done without dialogue. The extensions called may still be focused on one player, but both characters need to be affected by it. Let's say that character A is carrying a heavy object when "extend the weight" is called. The choice is obvious that A will now struggle more and more under the weight as it gets heavier and heavier. The focus is clearly on A.

What we want to avoid is having character B fall into the role of the passive observer where they stand around until A is done (when continue is called). The second character can assist in the extending by either contributing or contrasting. Using the heavy weight example from above, let's now look at these possible extensions:

Contribute
1. B callously piles more weight onto A.
2. B stands at the ready because A is beginning to teeter, contributing to the danger of the situation. The focus is on A because if danger

does befall someone, it will be A. Note that the action taken by B is observation, but is made aggressive by heightening the intent of being there for A, "just in case."

3. B is also carrying a heavy object with an "I feel your pain" kind of expression. B wants to make sure to fuel A's sorrow rather than victimize themselves too much.

4. B makes A's task more difficult by setting up obstacles. Perhaps a game is played of "Gee, that heavy object would look great over here. On second thought..."

Contrast

1. While A is struggling with the heavy objects, B walks back and forth in the background carrying heavy objects with ease. The objects can get bigger to include miming pianos, elephants, etc.

2. B is reclining in a lawn chair reading the paper. Occasionally, B looks over at A long enough to make a wincing face that says "My, but I would not try lifting that!"

In that last possibility, B is once again an observer but is not passive. He's active by commenting physically on the action that A is performing. A should be allowed to have his moment and by reacting, B is heightening that moment. If I am telling you a story that causes you to gasp, I might now make the story more scandalous or more horrifying or more wondrous to elicit more of that reaction. You are thus providing a reading for me to guide my storytelling.

In calling the extensions of the two-person exercise, it is good to test the performers by focusing your call on one player to see how the other reacts. Make sure that your call includes the player's name, so that your direction is clear. As before, you can also call for general extensions on scene aspects such as mood, relationship or use of environment. This may result in each player extending the aspect in a different way. If, for example, when calling an extension of the mood, one character becomes more angry while the other becomes more frightened, this can be golden. What has developed is a deeper dynamic than if both players were on the same page emotionally. Neither player should feel the need to adapt and you should not feel the need to correct one of them. Let the difference in readings play its course and a great relationship will develop. Just like Austin and Lee in Sam Shepard's *True West* or Gus and Ben in Harold Pinter's *The Dumb Waiter*, the scene will revolve around two characters in the same boat but reacting to the situation differently. The reality of the situation is not being denied—they are just playing out alternative takes on it.

Applying this to multi-person scenework, it is best to focus on one of the characters with your sidecoaching, allowing all the other characters to build off that one idea. Rather than tossing out another sidecoach to one of the other players, continue with the one focus, encouraging them to continue reacting. It will keep the scene less chaotic and give them better tools toward playing off their partners in the future.

THE ADAPTIVE IMPROVISER

The adaptive improviser is someone who takes the positive trait of wanting to support their fellow improviser, but goes too far. It is usually at the expense of the character that they have created and happens either within the first ten seconds of the scene or at a peak in the conflict of the scene. Support in improv is a wonderful thing and by no means am I suggesting that it be minimized, but on occasion it does get misdirected.

Let's say A and B enter a scene where A is performing an activity and whistling happily when B starts sobbing uncontrollably. Nine times out of ten, A will stop his activity, let their happiness drop and focus on B and what their character needs. Why? There is this thought in improv that certain types of choices are stronger and demand automatic focus. Though the scene is less than a minute old we have attached rules to the world created based on "what happens in real life." This creates a shorthand for the improv where certain cause and effect relationships are givens. I know many people who are annoyingly upbeat, regardless of the circumstances just as I know people who are overly melodramatic and whose "tragedies" need to be taken with a grain of salt. If A were to be persistently happy regardless of B's emotion, this is not denying B's reality, as some are taught. B's emotion is real for the character and we have to take the reasons as truth (let's say that B's dog has gone missing). A is providing a different take on the situation that now creates more depth in the scene. If A stays happy, offering platitudes and pithy advice to cheer up B, new options for the relationship become available. Perhaps

A and B are roommates and A did away with the dog that was driving him crazy, the dog that was chewing up his expensive shoes and waking him up early every morning with its howling. Perhaps A is playing a trick on B as revenge for something that happened in the past. Perhaps A has taken the dog to get an expensive grooming and wants to surprise B with it. None of these options are unrealistic.

What makes a choice strong and realistic is commitment. As we saw in the Extend/Continue exercise, anything can be expanded, and in doing so we give it resonance in the scene and significance in the character. Knowing that a character is happy is a wonderful, valid offer. Knowing that a character is happy even when others are miserable is levels above that.

Another myth that leads to adaptive improvising is that someone made an important plot choice quicker. This comes up especially with physical choices. A and B step forward, A making a choice, for instance, to be cooking something on the stove in the scene while B is throwing out a fishing line. They have an awkward moment looking at each other and then one of them drops what they are doing to take on a more complementary activity choice. Once again, the players are limiting their options. Rather than allow for these "mistakes" to develop into quirks that the scene can extend, they adapt as if the audience never saw it. The scene could easily have someone cooking on a fishing boat or someone practicing how to cast a line while in the kitchen. This is one of the virtues of an artform with no scripts, sets or costumes. The piece at hand is malleable and can be shaped in any direction imaginable. Once again, this is shorthand taking over. Fishing only happens on a fishing boat and cooking only happens in the kitchen. Give a location of an office and the chair goes downstage (usually downstage left) where the player sits and immediately starts typing at a computer. A location of a restaurant leads to two chairs being placed center stage at a three-quarters angle to each other. Risks are eliminated in order to get to the task at hand faster. And if two people move quickly, simultaneously, one of the players hits their restart button thinking it doesn't register with the audience.

A subtler example of adaptive improvising is what I term the *improv boxstep*. This happens at the top of the scene where three people step out of a back line to do a scene and one of the improvisers instinctively goes back. What is going through his mind is that there are two people to a scene and anything more than that gets too confusing. Or she is thinking that her idea could not possibly work with what the other actors are about to do. This is the quickest self-condemnation ever.

This is one of the reasons we used the one-minute scenes in the previous chapter. The first minute can give you a sense of the direction in which the scene will go if the reality created in those moments is adhered to until the end of the scene. A rehearsal is greatly benefited by doing drills of one-minute scenes or Opening Lines (where two actors step forward and do the first three lines of a scene, each one taking a line in turn). This helps the performers vary their choices, strengthen their choices, and, most importantly, recognize their initial choices. This will not eliminate the adaptive improviser but does minimize its frequency.

We also see these swift adaptations in the peaks of conflict. Characters who were previously steadfast in their attitudes or beliefs now have a huge transformation because they feel their scene partner's needs call for it. In the lost dog scene, there may come a point where B is so dismayed about the lost dog that the character threatens suicide. A, who has still been whistling happily up to this point, now shifts emotionally and tries to talk B down from the ledge. This is a perfectly valid choice, but is it a character choice or is it one player (A) doing what they think is supposed to happen? Those "supposed to happen" choices are rarely inspired and often forced. If A kept being happy in spite of B's suicidal tendencies, would that be unrealistic? Not if A was secretly trying to get rid of B all along (similar to how Charles Boyer is trying to drive Ingrid Bergman crazy in *Gaslight*). Not if B is melodramatic and always threatens suicide (look at Christopher Durang's *Baby with the Bathwater* and you will see a sequence of scenes where miscarriage is handled more and more lightly).

Some improvisers think there is supposed to be some big transformation in the characters in order for the scene to be valid (if this were so, then no Beckett play would be valid). Thoughts like this are monitors of the audience more than the character. They are no longer feeling what the character feels and are making choices based on what they think the audience wants to see happen. This shortchanges the possibilities in a scene. The audience tends to regard scenes in relation to what they are familiar with. They are not averse to new takes or surprising twists. They just don't think ahead in that way. That is why they are not performers themselves.

The point is that there are no givens in a scene except one: the first thing a player does in a scene is the first thing that the scene is built upon. It is not a time filler until something "important" happens. It cannot be erased because the other player made a "bigger" choice. Most of all, there is no way that it cannot fit with the other player's choice regardless of how "strange" the juxtaposition may look.

All those thoughts are part of the myths that exist in improvisation. As a director, you want to be in the position of empowering your troupe and that means not looking at the scenes in these contexts. Each scene creates its own context and this happens within the first few moves. Even when the players don't recognize that, you should have your sights on it.

Look at any sketch that you see on television or stage. Each sets its premise up quickly to allow for the build. Look at the initial scene in most plays. They set the mood early on, which drives the piece. The scenery, lighting, costuming and characterizations all contribute to establishing the information you need through which to view this particular world. Look at the beginning of *Hamlet*. The play opens on the guard platform of Elsinore castle. It is dark. It is quiet. We witness a conversation between two soldiers:

> Bernardo: Who's there?
>
> Francisco: Nay, answer me. Stand and unfold yourself.
>
> Bernardo: Long live the King!
>
> Francisco: Bernardo?

Here Shakespeare starts to unfold information on the wars that serve as a backdrop to the play, while also setting a mood of uneasiness. The soldiers are on edge and unsure to the point where they are on guard, even in the presence of those who are familiar to them. If this were an improv scene, however, this would be disregarded in place of finding "what the scene is about." Within a few lines Horatio enters and the jumpiness and questions begin again. The first few lines have established both Bernardo and Francisco's attitudes toward the world around them. In an improv scene,

Horatio's entrance might wipe away what happened before. Shakespeare, however, has made simple choices for the opening and allows the play to unfold to grander themes along the way.

The adaptive improviser is not incapable of making choices. They let their commitment to those choices wane in the face of other choices made. These commitments can turn on a dime, making them extremely difficult to catch in sidecoaching. Some directors will stop a scene and try to rewind to a moment where something was dropped. This offers mixed results. When you try to go back to the moment it is never the same. The energy is different, possibly an energy of wanting to get things right this time or an energy of self-consciousness. Possibly the players are able to resume the scene without a problem. Nonetheless, the act of redoing does little to train the actors what to do in future scenes when the commitment wanes. If you do redo a scene, try not doing the same scene but a new scene with similar elements. If we were to stop the lost dog scene when A conforms to B's needs after the subject of suicide has come up, we would simply have the players do a new scene that involves strongly contrasting emotions. That was the commitment issue after all. [Note: This is different from when we discussed redoing short scenes in the previous chapter. In that case, we were focusing on choices and challenging the actors to make those same choices so that they could embrace them more fully. The goal of challenges is to help the players make big choices, whereas the goal of sidecoaching should be focused on drawing attention to the choices as they are being made so they don't get easily lost.]

Stopping scenes can undermine confidence and should be done sparingly. Also, actors need to learn how to maneuver through failing scenes and to learn how to save themselves in future performances. As a director, you see where the scene did work and you want to reinforce that. This can be done in different ways:

1. *Affirm choices before they get lost.* You know which players lose focus or which ones bend. Sidecoaching does not have to be just about correcting people. When I am directing a scene and one of the characters says something that really clues me in to what that character, relationship or scene dynamic is about, I will sometimes sidecoach them to repeat it. The choice will have more resonance

and will be less often dropped in the course of the scene. After the player repeats the statement, I sometimes follow with, "That is your mantra." Labeling it that way allows me to call for it later in the scene if I feel the character has lost their want or attitude. This is particularly helpful at those peak moments of conflict where adapting tends to happen most.

2. *Call for a reconnect.* In some cases, the initial choice was connected to a specific aspect of the scene that can be revisited, such as the environment, a specific activity or mimed prop. For example, a nervous character may exhibit the need to light a new cigarette. Call to resume that activity and that may revive a lost attitude, mood or emotion.

3. *Soundtracking.* Layering music on top of the scene can provide a great connection to any emotional choice that has subsided and inspire it to build farther. Soundtracking can be done vocally as well as with a musician and is a great tool for improvisers to use in a show.

4. *Send in the reinforcements.* Use the other members of the troupe to reincorporate scene elements. If B has switched into a happy mood even though the dog is still lost, send another player in with the dog's corpse. The members should make a quick entrance and exit. Otherwise, the scene might get too complicated. You may be tempted to enter the scene yourself. This can work as long as the offer made is all about endowing one of the players on stage, though you want to do this as infrequently as possible. It helps to delegate the other players to keep things professional and to train others in support work.

Keep in mind that many performers need to be prepared for when they are going to be sidecoached. A sudden call from the sidelines during a scene can damage whatever tenuous commitment they had. Prior to any scene, introduce the idea and stress the need to stay in the moment.

CHAPTER 7: CREATING A FORMAT WITH YOUR TROUPE

When Del Close created the structure of the Harold, he created with it the idea of finding the game, an alternative to Second City's tradition of creating scenarios to improvise through, or using Spolin's game work. It was a new way to approach scenework.

There is an ever-growing body of work that is about altering the approach. The performances that I have witnessed or been a part of have included shows aiming to be fast and furious, to use as few words as possible, to copy the rhythms of jazz, to play with long drawn-out "real life" scenes, or to portray erotic content. These are qualities that the separate shows aimed for that were not attached to any particular set theatrical happening (such as a need to open with a monologue or to have a set of second beats) but rather create a set vocabulary of options to pull from.

Throughout my improv career, I have done a number of different formats. For the first few years, they were borrowed structures taken from books or from watching other troupes perform. We all go through these stages of appropriation, whether it is picking apart shortform games that we have seen on *Whose Line...?* or doing the Harold directly as written in *Truth In Comedy*. This is a natural default for any troupe. It is a part of creating a zone of comfort from which to play and when the format is all figured out for you, it takes a lot of weight off the group's shoulders. At some point, however, these formats can lose their charm or, even worse, their purpose. A troupe will eventually need to explore their own approach of structuring a performance.

Sometimes, the fit was not so good to begin with. I have seen many troupes do a Harold because it was what was out there, relying solely on the reading to fill them in on what to do. As a result, the cast is working hard to satisfy the needs of the form rather than the other way around. The Harold, while a wonderful format that can be masterfully handled by players who understand it, becomes an albatross for those who do it because they feel they are "supposed to" in order to progress. There is no killjoy as big as obligation when it comes to performing. And when the taking on of a new form is only supported by third-person accounts educated by reading material, the endeavour has less of a chance.

Other groups outgrow the forms they know. Many have followed a path from shortform to longform structure to freeform because the newer idea offered new possibilities. This is part of the natural cycle of artistic invention. Picasso was a highly schooled artist before he ventured into the unique direction of Cubism, as inspired by Cézanne. All art is a balance of the new and borrowed, but that which the artists borrow still give some selfish satisfaction which the personal modifications build upon.

Among the structures that I have helped create was Doppelgangers, an improvised play where each of the actors would improvise in a different playwright genre simultaneously. While working with NY Theatresports, I workshopped Hyperlinks, an internet-inspired improvisation where the audience would control the editing. Both of these formats had markers that were hit along the way to help maintain the arc of the piece, like a specific story structure to follow, or a set opening involving monologues. Sometimes there were theatrical devices that were specific to the formats that were employed. For example, in Lifeline, my troupe Hiatus would scatter improvised answering machine messages throughout the piece as a way to develop the characters.

There were some shows that had no format whatsoever. Instead, the focus was on varying the approach of the work. With *imp.* my partner Karen Wight and I found a way to improvise vignettes using as few words as possible. The form had no theatrical devices to employ or markers to guide where the narrative was to go. The rehearsal process involved an exploration of new ways to communicate a story physically.

Each of these formats appealed to my very personal tastes or philosophies. In this chapter, we will talk about creating formats and approaches based on the visions in your head.

EXPLORING THE WORLD AROUND YOU

The world is full of inspiration for you to pull from—not just in the performing arts but by crossing over into the worlds of science, sculpture, sociology and architecture, among others. Piet Mondrian created a series of paintings through mathematics. Alan Moore wrote graphic novels inspired by and structured on religious tenets. There are unlimited possibilities for your work as well. What inspires you outside improv? When you do improv, where do you have the most fun? Creating characters? Playing with the audience?

I have a list of theatrical aspects that I use in imagining new forms, that comes from working with NY Theatresports. Theatresports is an improvised competition between two teams of players who issue challenges to each other at the top of each round of shortform games. We were given a list of possible challenges, a thorough breakdown of the different aspects of game playing which provided a good way to categorize the current repertoire of shortform structures and a good starting point for developing new ones. Here is that list of aspects with examples of shortform and longform formats that focus on each. (For more details on the formats listed, check out *The Art of Chicago Improv* for longform descriptions and *Impro for Storytellers* for the shortform. You can also find information online at the Chicago Improv Network Wiki and The Improv Encyclopedia.)

Aspect	Shortform example	Longform example
Character	• World's Worst	• La Ronde • Sybil
Environment	• Emotional Zones	• Close Quarters • Monoscene
Music/Poetry	• Poet's Corner • Sing It!	• Beatbox • Improvised Musical
Emotion	• Oscar-Winning Moments	• Soap Opera
Genre	• Directed Authors	• Documentary • Movie
Narrative	• Typewriter	• Campfire • Spoon River
Physicality	• Slideshow • Sit, Stand, Kneel	• Organic improv

Using the Audience	• Puppets/Moving Bodies	• L'Esprit d'Escalier
Using the Whole Team	• Freeze Tag	applicable to any format
Time Warp any restrictions given on the way time is used	• ding!/New Choice • Forward Reverse	• Eventé • Moebius
Word Warp any language-related restrictions	• Entrances and Exits	• Silent Movie
Giving up Control any restrictions placed on the actors	• Any guessing game (also known as Naive Games) • Actor's Nightmare	• Hyperlinks
Theme	• Rashomon	• Deconstruction

Many confuse the technical side of the piece with what the piece is about. For instance, editing is not really an improvisational aspect. It is a means by which to explore new environments or to time warp.

EXAMPLE 1: WORKING FROM AN ASPECT

Let's say that your group loves to work on Character. The aspect of Character can be explored many different ways:

1. having people play many different characters

2. playing well-known characters in different contexts

3. having characters inspired by the audience in different ways

4. having one character shown from different viewpoints

Just taking one of those ideas and improvising scenes around it will create an instant shortform structure and show directions to follow for a longer format. Let's look at the idea of having people play many different characters in a format, for instance. In doing it, we want to be as specific as possible in the parameters. I would direct two actors to do a scene where each starts out as one character and when I call an actor's name, he must enter as a different character and go back and forth between the two. This is a straightforward challenge that has potential for mistakes. Mistakes are wonderful in development. How easily does the actor differ between the two characters? We can challenge them to make their characters extreme physically or vocally. How easily does the actor move between the two characters? Maybe we need to create a vocabulary to make that transition clearer to an audience.

It helps to play a few scenes in a row with different people before applying any notes or challenges. The player's natural tendencies, regardless of their experience level, when taking on a new idea is invaluable in developing a format in which he can excel. Unless you see the improvisers second-guessing or holding back too early on in the process, let them run free with their own interpretations. This is where we will be pleasantly surprised.

Once we have a good sense of how the concept works in one scene, we can start building into longer formats. Again, we can refer to the aspects list. For instance, if we have just done a two-person scene where each actor has played two characters, we can then take one of these directions:

1. Environment—Transposing the characters to a different location may provide new discoveries, such as doing a multi-character scene in a more confined location, such as an elevator or a lifeboat.

2. Narrative—Try making a specific choice as to which character to follow into the next scene. For instance, imagine Player A plays Character 1 and 2 with Player B who plays Character 3 and 4 and in the next scene, Player B plays Character 3 and 4 with Player C who provides two new characters.

3. Time Warp—We can play with jumping to different times in the characters' stories, even showing them at different ages.

4. Giving up Control—We can base which characters the actors play and the transitions between them upon the whim of the director or the audience.

This is now creating a vocabulary for the format. Now it is just a matter of playing and replaying the format to find where it works best or is the most fun.

EXAMPLE 2: CONCEPTUAL INSPIRATIONS
When adapting an idea that is not automatically performance-ready (which

we will refer to as an "abstract"), like a love of chess, we want to match up the appealing facets of the abstract with theatrical aspects. For example:

1. The specific movements of the pieces can be translated into set entrances or transitions in the format (environment/give up control) affecting how and when people enter scenes.

2. Chess is full of archetypes (kings, pawns, etc.) that can be developed as characters similar to the characters in Commedia.

3. There are strategies to a game of chess. How can the rules of taking out pieces translate to onstage dynamics?

4. Ultimately, the goal is to capture the king. If one player were the king of the game, what improvisational ways could you attempt to "capture" him?

My format Hyperlinks was inspired by my enjoyment of the internet and how disparate worlds could be connected through various links. Entering the keyword of "spirit" on a search engine would bring up websites on the supernatural, aged alcohol and cheerleading tournaments. This idea of instant connections based on thematic ideas was easily relatable to improvisation, but the question was what the structure would look like.

My first decision was to let the audience have complete control over the show to mirror the experience of websurfing in how people would wander from link to link on various whims. The result was that scenes would vary in length throughout the show—from several minutes down to several seconds—as the audience would signal edits by yelling "click." On this cue, the players would have to jump to a new scene based on whatever was just "clicked" on, whether an action, sound or piece of dialogue. It was a simple device that would allow the audience to communicate clearly with the players. Once again, the edit is not the structure here; the audience control is, which brings up the issue of how the show would begin and end, particularly maintaining an arc to the piece. Thus was born the "bread-and-butter" scene.

Based on a suggestion of a word from the audience, three monologists would step forward and, in mimicking the list that comes up on a search engine, do the first two lines of a character monologue related to the suggestion. The audience is prompted to pick one of the monologists who then starts at the beginning of their monologue and goes beyond the two lines they have already done. Meanwhile, the other players create still tableaus of the story being relayed. From that point forward the audience clicks, cueing the monologist to tag their way into or add themselves to the tableau which then comes to life. This "bread-and-butter" scene would have the strongest grounding since it would have a strong central character—personal websites tend to be obsessive, passionate expressions of character—making it easy to return to the storyline. These recurrences would give the show a place to build so that the show would not be completely tangential to itself, though other stories would be reincorporated as well.

EXAMPLE 3: ADAPTATION

When Christopher Nolan's *Memento* came out, not only did it shake the filmmaking world with its original cinematic techniques, it immediately sparked inspiration in hundreds of improvisers who became obsessed with the idea of an improvised version of the movie.

Creating an improv format seems easier when you are working directly from source material. The process of adaptations involves establishing solid markers and/or foundations. To a certain degree you know where the story is going in each performance. On the downside, to a certain degree you know where the story is going in each performance. There is a fine line between developing a helpful skeleton for a show and restricting yourself creatively within a confining structure.

An improvised *Memento* would be all about the foundation, with some focus on creating markers. The foundation is where we learn about the main characters, their backgrounds, and the environment they are in. This information would dictate where we would jump to from five minutes before (an arbitrary amount of time for the sake of this example). If there were two characters discussing the woman they were both in love with, we might have her in the following scene (which chronologically takes place before the first scene) doing or saying something that would cause them to have that conversation after she leaves.

At the start of each scene, markers will be created. These are clearly marked transition points. If one scene begins with one character drawing a gun on the other, we know when we jump back in time that the next scene will end with the gun being pulled; we know what we are leading up to.

Adaptation structures can suffer from having the actors working toward set markers, giving them a feeling of being too timed out. This is most evident in improvised murder mysteries where we know who the victim is and then must hold off on the murder until the right time. Then, we have to hold off on revealing the murder until the very end. As a result, you have players who make less than bold choices because too radical an action would throw off the focus of the show. Imagine if we instead did NOT know who was going to be murdered. We get a suggestion from the audience of an event (an engagement party, for instance) where the players just focus on the dynamics between all players. They improvise tensions and friendships until the lights go out, during which one of the characters is murdered. This frees up the cast a lot more to do whatever they want.

Kenn Adams, who I worked with in Freestyle Repertory Theater, developed a structure for improvising two-act plays. Being a playwright as well, he mined his experience (also using *Playwriting* by Bernard Grebanier as a reference) to find what the commonalities were between most plays, focusing specifically on those that unfolded linearly. In the end, Kenn had created the Story Spine, an arc with specific "events" that occur along the way, that could be used in improvising based on plays, movies or novels.

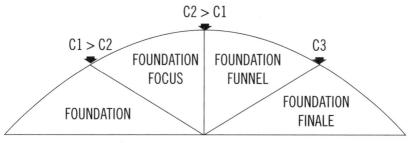

Story Spine structure developed by Kenn Adams.

The first commonality he decided upon was that there would be a definite protagonist and antagonist which would be referred to as Character 1 and Character 2. Most stories revolve around a single conflict between two people. Even huge conflicts such as the fight between good and evil in *Star Wars* would not have been appreciated as much had both sides not been represented by the figures of Luke Skywalker and Darth Vader. This established a clear arc to follow—the conflict between two main characters.

During the **Foundation**, characters, environments and histories are introduced until we reach the **First Significant Event** where one character takes a direct action toward another (C1 > C2). This action can be proclaiming their love, threatening their life, stealing their money, etc., but both parties need to be present for it to be significant. For instance, Character 1 cannot proclaim his love for Character 2 to a third person even though it's a big piece of new information. In *Casablanca*, the movie starts with a map of the world, focusing on the passage between Spain and Morocco. Soon, it focuses on the streets of Casablanca where we see someone shot down in front of a nationalist poster. We hear a police radio announcement of missing letters of transit. Then the focus narrows even more to Rick's Bar where we see transactions at the different tables between people trying to get out of the country. Several minutes pass before we meet Rick, played by Humphrey Bogart, our first main character and even longer before we meet Ingrid Bergman's Ilsa. The significant moment is when Ilsa has Sam play *that* song, "As Time Goes By," because even if unintentional, it provokes Rick to emerge from the back in a dark mood when he realizes who has requested it. There are events that happen before that moment— the man shot in the street, Peter Lorré being dragged away—but none of them cause any ripples around them. They are treated as part of the routine of this world. But when that song plays, Rick goes against character. He is suddenly emotional, in contrast with his earlier stoicism. He sits with Ilsa, even though he had stated before that it was his policy to not sit with patrons. While there can be several events in the Foundation, it requires a strong reaction to make one significant.

Once the Significant Event has happened, it sets off a chain of events in the **Foundation Focus** until the **First Significant Repercussion**, where Character 2 is compelled to make a direct action toward Character 1 in return. The key word again is "significant." When Ilsa corners Rick at the club to get the letters of transit, she does everything she can, including pulling a gun, which we would normally consider to be significant. However, Rick has no response to any of her tactics and instead takes an action on his own terms, where he offers to help her leave Casablanca, as Ilsa breaks down.

This action will bring about **The Question** that the second act will now answer. To be most effective this question needs to a) be a simple yes or no question and b) mention both Characters. For example, if we look at the *Star Wars* trilogy as a whole, the first significant event is that Luke gets past Vader and destroys the Death Star that was important to the Dark Side's plans. This empowers the Rebels and sets in motion a series of consequences, until Darth Vader responds by confessing to Luke that he is his father (severing his hand as an added touch). You can see how both of these are significant events that stand apart from all other actions in the movies. Prior to Luke destroying the Death Star, Vader even comments on how he senses that the Force is stronger in Luke than in anyone he had encountered before. Luke, after learning who his father is, jumps down a vent—to kill himself or to escape, we don't know—changing his pattern throughout the movie, of being someone who doesn't back down from a fight. The question becomes, *Will Luke defeat Vader?* or maybe, *Will Luke join Vader on the Dark Side?* Not just join the Dark Side, but join Vader on the Dark Side. In *Casablanca*, the question is whether Rick will leave on that plane with Ilsa.

Now that the question is in the air, all characters try to answer it, picking sides and taking actions accordingly. In *Casablanca*, even Frenchie, with his bet as to whether Victor Laszlo will be able to get out of the country, is indirectly pushing for the central question to be answered *no*. He would benefit from Victor leaving on the plane with Ilsa, not Rick. As these moves to answer the question occur, we will come to **The Climax**, where one of our main characters takes an action toward a supporting character (Character 3) that will definitively answer the question, or set the answer in motion. When Emperor Palpatine lashes out directly at Luke at the end of *Return of the Jedi* rather than through Darth Vader, Vader gets to look at the situation from outside himself and makes the decision to help Luke by attacking Palpatine. This definitively answers both of the questions we imagined. No, Luke will not join Vader on the Dark Side, in fact it is going the other way. Yes, Luke will defeat Vader, or at least the Dark Side in him.

From this point, it is a matter of tying up loose ends in the **Finale**. Which can last one minute (in *Casablanca*, once Frenchie has gotten involved in covering up Major Strasser's death) or for a few more scenes (in *Jedi*, where we return to the Ewok Village to catch up on Leia's relationship with Luke and Han Solo).

What makes this structure work as an adaptation of play narratives is that what look like markers that need to be hit are actually new foundations that are introduced. The first significant event, for example, is not a set piece that you need to make happen at some point in the first quarter of the play. If that were the case, the improvisers would undoubtedly hold off on taking big actions for fear of hitting the crescendo too soon. Instead, this structure gives them the opportunity to take any action that has just happened and make it supremely significant. Similarly, the Foundation Focus builds off that significant event and the Foundation Funnel builds off the question that is raised.

In doing an improv adaptation, you want to make sure that the format serves you and not the other way around. A format that involves too many hoops to jump through—e.g., in scene 1 we need to meet the hero, in scene 2 we need to have the love interest, scene 3 we meet the hero, etc.— significantly holds back the troupe. It is like when you have a birthday and everyone gathers around to sing "Happy Birthday." The group inevitably falls into the tempo of the slowest singer. When you have an overly structured format, no one wants to zoom ahead in fear that someone will be left behind or things will get confused or there will be nothing else to do once that point is hit. The group will end up following the slowest choices.

EXAMPLE 4: CREATING AN ENVELOPE

An *envelope* is a show structure made up of smaller self-contained components. The most well-known envelopes are competition-themed formats such as Theatresports, ComedySportz and Micetro. Rather than do a straight rundown of games with nothing but intros in between, there is now an arc that builds throughout the show, of teams or individuals competing for points. The audience gets to enjoy some improv and also witnesses the victory of one team over another, like at any sports event. Envelopes like this are helpful in keeping a flow in a show that could otherwise be riddled with stops and starts. It makes it feel like more of an event for the audience.

Competitions are only one way to create this arc. Any theme can be applied because all themes come with a conflict that can build. Years ago, my troupe Hiatus created The Lost Land of Hiatus, where through improvisation we would fully invent an ancient civilization, the Hiatians. The first of the two acts would explore specific facets of the culture through specially crafted games. For example, audience members would be asked to draw very quickly on large sheets of paper that would later be "discovered" as cave paintings that illustrated a Hiatian ritual. Later in the show, an audience member's dream would be reinterpreted into a narrated dream ballet that would explain the Hiatians' creation myth. The second act would compile all this new information into a short improvised play that took place in this civilization.

Whatever the idea is, keep it simple. One envelope I was involved in creating was very convoluted and the audience couldn't make sense of it. The premise was that the audience was aboard a spaceship from an alien planet on its way to Earth and the games we were playing were glimpses at the typical lives of Earthlings. We were being overly clever, and if we had fewer levels to the concept (while the individual games can be more complicated) the audience and players would have had a better time. Keeping the concept to a single arc that can be defined in one sentence (two teams of improvisers compete for points, a crew of anthropologists discover information about a lost civilization, etc.) is a good way to guarantee simplicity and fun.

When your arc is in place, you can then fit the games in, but beware of shoehorning them into place. This happens most of all when troupes grow attached to a game, thinking it is their signature game. The point of creating a format, even an envelope that relies on established games, is that you want to try something new. The show fulfills the needs of the troupe and the games fulfill the needs of the show. Reverse this notion and you might as well not bother.

THE MERITS OF BEING SELFISH

What I'm into doing on stage surely isn't for everyone, but I enjoy it, it is what I'm compelled to do.

—Shira Piven

Onstage, selfishness can be the most destructive factor in a troupe's performance. In creating that show, however—the format, the games, or the approach—you most definitely start your process by being selfish. In fact, you should embrace it. It is nice to say that the performance is for the audience, but it is not true, unless you are on a gig at a pediatric cancer ward or doing a show for the elderly or the homeless. You are first and foremost performing for yourself. It drives you. It speaks to you. It feeds you. Show appreciation for the audience at all times—they are paying you the honor of coming to see your show above everything else they could be doing—but do not create the show for them. Don't blame them when the show doesn't work and don't create the show for them.

Performances, particularly improvisational performances, come from a place of exploration, a "wouldn't-this-be-cool-to-try" feeling that is fun to pursue and selfish. This is the basis for all great work. Everything comes across as pretentious in its effort to be "groundbreaking," or feels flat in its attempt to make a statement that "needs to be made." If you personally need to make the statement, go for it. Otherwise, just leave it alone. You are not doing anyone any favors by going into a show looking to "blow people's minds." This is the demon of forced uniqueness peeking up its head and it needs to be knocked back down before it infects your project with pretention and obligations. Neither are fun to watch or perform.

Now let us take this newly embraced selfishness and use it. Find what it is that you enjoy, you are inspired by, or what you do well, and exploit it fully. Once you have made the major decisions regarding the project, then you may begin adapting it for audience perspective, making the transitions clearer, fine-tuning the opening to make it easier to get suggestions. Whatever the case may be, it will be easier to make a show more palatable to others once you have your own stakes in it figured out.

The best examples of seflishly created formats are those created for solo improvisation. Currently, there are two prominent types of solo improv formats. On the one hand, you have several unconnected character monologues. The other is any variation on the Sybil format invented by Andy Eninger where one person performs a series of scenes playing the multiple characters within each scene. Because these are the most known of the one-person formats out there, new solo performers are plugging themselves into one of the two regardless of the fit. Truly, solo improv should reflect the individual performer.

> I personally believe there are no schools of improv, we're all our own school of improv, so your solo piece is the ultimate expression of that school.
>
> —*Jill Bernard*

When I directed my wife Adrianne Frost in her solo show Wonderworm, it made sense that she would be doing a series of character monologues. Her greatest strength as an improviser is her ability to do very fully developed characters. In directing her, I just had to help her find the arc for each monologue which meant developing a new skill.

When I worked with Phil Incorvia on his one-man improv show, the first step was rethinking the format entirely. Phil was performing a Sybil variation despite his discomfort with doing different characters. Those familiar with the Sybil realize that unless the characters are distinct from each other, the piece becomes harder for the audience to follow. When I caught Phil's show, I noticed immediately that the piece was strongest not when he was playing the characters in the scene but when he was providing background and details as narrator. Phil is a very intellectual performer and could have focused a show around just that but was instead caught up in what he thought a solo show required and what he thought the audience wanted to see. In the end, we devised an improvised format structured like a college-style seminar where he would create origin stories of common English phrases suggested by the audience. The format connected directly to what Phil enjoyed doing (he happened to major in Anthropology in college) and the show was brilliant to watch.

Here are some other examples of improvised solo shows that are custom-made for their performers:

1. Jill Bernard's <u>Drum Machine</u> is a Sybil variation with a more punk approach thanks to its use of percussion-backed vocals and edgy presentation which revolves around an audience suggestion of an historical era where the story takes place.

2. Ian Roberts' <u>Lazy Man</u> is almost an anti-one-man show, going through the solo performance conventions of relaying personal stories while keeping it unscripted. The title alone conveys the tone of the concept.

3. Jonathan Appel, an acclaimed director of improvised films, has done a wide variety of solo formats. One show was inspired by Tom Cruise's megalomaniacal character in *Magnolia*. In this show, Jonathan led a seminar where he would share secrets with the audience with heavy interaction on how to be a "great improviser" like himself.

If an improviser is looking to go solo, it should be based on what that performer can exploit and showcase about themselves. Group formats are the same.

ADAPTING A FORMAT

Sometimes when a form demands too many gimmicks and demands too many things and too many changes, too many edits, too many things like that, there isn't that time, there isn't that empty space. I really think that empty space is what you give performers, enough empty space and you just put them out there, leave them out there for a bit. Now they have to do something with it. I like things that are more the responsibility of the performer versus the performer following a dance.

—Armando Diaz

It's too easy to immediately dismiss a format idea the first time it is tried. But if after repeated rehearsals a certain edit, device or any other piece of the production doesn't click with the cast, excise it. Give it enough room to be explored fully, but then take care of your performers by pulling out the things that get in their way.

The format is secondary to the improv. Making a structure too sacred only serves to make it harder to play. After all, we improvise for the fun of it. When that gets hindered, you need to step back and recalculate what is supremely necessary and what can be changed in or removed from the structure.

There is a tendency to add new rules to safeguard against failure, but it is more effective to scale back the parameters that are already in place. Many issues arise in an attempt to satisfy the needs of the format and if those obligations are removed, rather than to add more obligations, it will allow the improvisers to not be as distracted by what is supposed to happen. Instead, they can focus on where they are in the moment.

Many times the format is never truly complete until it has had a run in front of an audience. There is no way around it and striving to perfect the structure before opening night is a pipe dream. Sometimes, you will only learn how well the form works with audience participation. As mentioned earlier, the audience was in complete control during a Hyperlinks show. This meant training the performers in doing a string of three-second scenes in case any patrons decided to abuse their power. Suprisingly though, there was a common psychology in the audiences we encountered. There was always a hesitancy at the beginning of the shows as the audience slowly shook its reticence to use its newfound editing power. When it did, the momentum built quickly. Then at around forty-five minutes in—the running time of the show was an hour—they would start to pull back. Instinctively, they knew to let us have time to develop scenes at the beginning, keep the energy going in the middle, and then have time to wrap up scenes at the end. There was no way of knowing this would happen without putting the show up and trusting it would all work out.

The biggest question for troupes is always whether the audience will enjoy it. Even though we are allowing ourselves to be selfish, we still realize that we are entertainers.

You cannot predict what the audience will enjoy. Their tastes will differ and are constantly changing. Popular culture is full of examples of horrible movies and television shows that were made because the producers thought they were a sure thing. In the end, there are expensive special effects vehicles that bomb because they had no substance or television shows that had a celebrity attached and nothing else. The public is fickle but will find what they want to see. Your audience will find your show. Making the audience believe that is part of marketing and marketing has nothing to do with the construction of the format.

While you do not have control over what the audience will like, you do have control over how strong your product is and that is a much more productive focus for you to have. You even have a say in how much the audience understands of what's going on. This is most relevant when dealing with new transition techniques. Will the audience get that the one character is being played by two different actors at different ages? Will they understand when we have jumped in time? Without the visual information of costuming or set changes that would normally clue the audience in, the responsibility falls on the players' shoulders.

Many times the audience understands more than we give them credit for. The truth is that spectators tend to put things in their own context. Fifty people can look at the same abstract painting and see fifty different images. It's the same when they watch a scene. If the actors don't establish the specifics of their relationship, then the audience will assume one. Sometimes, when they don't get a piece of information until it's presented somewhere down the road, it shifts the piece into a new context that is enjoyable to watch.

If there is certain information that absolutely needs to come across, try a short set where whatever information is conveyed in the transitions is exaggerated. If there is a time jump that shows a character aging, do it to a ridiculous degree. This will show what the actors are together on as far as what is being portrayed to the audience. As you do more sets, tone down the exaggeration. If the actors are still agreeing on where the scene is transitioning to, then the audience will most likely not have any problems either.

THE SUGGESTION

> If it was up to Keith [Johnstone] we wouldn't take any suggestions, we would just start improvising, because at the end of the day, it's either entertaining or interesting or it's not, and the fact that it's improvised is true, but we're never going to prove it to everybody.
>
> —Dan O'Connor

It used to be a given that any improv show begins with an audience suggestion, also referred to as a *get*. The purpose for many is to directly involve the audience in the performance while subconsciously satisfying the need to prove to them that the show is in fact improvised. For me, a get helps give an agreed-upon starting point that minimizes the chaotic din in the cast's minds. Without this, improv scenes sometimes meander until they hit a nugget that they can agree to build from. Getting a suggestion related to plot specifics can help a cast that gets reticent to jump to the meat of the scene sooner, where they can focus on other aspects of the improvisation.

The suggestion is no longer mandatory and is sometimes even considered a burden. One set that I saw at the Chicago Improv Festival started with "May we have a suggestion that we will then ignore for the next thirty minutes."

One of the most common reasons that groups eschew the use of suggestions is the task that comes from incorporating it "successfully" or making it relevant to the piece. This results in the get becoming too involved in the plot. For example, the word "fondue" will usually inspire little outside of scenes of a couple eating fondue and chances are someone will burn themselves on it before the scene is over.

If you choose to incorporate audience suggestions into the format you have just created, it should be the last piece of the puzzle. Formats such as Harolds or freeforms can use any suggestion, but when the format is more structure-specific, it can create more hoops to jump through. During the format's creation, you should determine what the best starting point is, i.e., there is a central character, so getting information about her in the suggestion will help build the momentum.

Improvisers have long been cultivating how to get suggestions. They have learned that when you ask for a relationship you will get the suggestion of lovers or brothers, but when you ask for "a way two people know each other," it opens up a broader range of possibilities. Asking for a strange way they know each other opens it up a little more.

Another way is to take suggestions is without a question-and-answer approach. Here are some varied ways that I have seen the audience incorporated into the improvisation:

- gathering personal objects that are used as props
- using a photo ID as an idea for a character mask
- giving them a reading using tarot cards for a suggestion of themes
- throwing a dart at a board of suggestions

This is not just about being different—that would be gratuitous and pretentious—but about catching the audience off-guard. The audience can get in their heads during a performance too. If they are called upon for a suggestion, they start to wonder if they should be funny or outrageous with their choice, especially if they happen to be another improviser.

Throwing them into an activity, one that doesn't immediately telegraph how it relates to the show as a whole, takes the pressure off them to be clever or special.

PREPARING FOR THE SLUMP OR THE EARLY PEAK

In every group, there comes a time to shake things up. When you work hard at something you can easily fall into routines that become counterproductive when you are trying to be creative. This is different from the idea of ritual that we discussed in *Building an Ensemble*. When someone goes to church on a weekly basis to maintain their connection with God, that is an example of ritual. Ritual has purpose. When the purpose is nothing more than completing the task of going to church on a weekly basis, it has become routine, drained of faith. If this can happen with faith, it most definitely can happen with your craft.

For whatever reason, you may find your troupe spinning its wheels. This is a widespread doldrum that occurs when there is little or no progress or there is an oversaturation of improv work being done. (Cases of an individual performer in an uninspired rut are addressed later in *Dealing with Issues Within Your Troupe*.)

This pattern is just like any we have discussed in creating challenges for players. Similarly, these patterns can be countered by a radical change in the process. The most obvious is taking time off from the project to reenergize, but there are many ways to shake up rehearsals.

- Consider working on formats that are completely different from whatever the project entails. When a group is too focused on getting a certain objective right, it makes that goal near impossible. Jumping to a different format can remove that concern of failure.

- Lead the group through something that isn't even related to improv. If there is a feeling developing that rehearsals are boring or a source of tension, find an activity that will create a new environment while fostering the group dynamic. Sing show tunes. Do some yoga. Ballroom dancing. Fencing. You could easily justify how the skills of any of these activities could apply to your work anyway.

- Change your tactics. If you do not have the time to go off lesson, find new ways to approach the lesson. Incorporate the viewing of movies, listening to music, playing board games (such as playing Clue in character to prepare for a murder mystery show), etc.

Inspiration is a diminishable commodity that needs renewing and as the director, you are its most reliable gauge. The feelings that block it cannot be simply waited out, ignored or disciplined away. They need to be fully countered or released.

DIRECTING A SPECIFIC PROJECT

Each show will have a central idea that will help prioritize what skills are most important. A stylized improvisation of a Mamet play will not require as much narrative work as an improvised Shakespeare show. A performance of a La Ronde (where a selection of characters rotate through two person scenes with each other) will focus more on character than edits. In working a new format, see what the new focus is as a way to start off a series of rehearsals.

In the summer of 2002, I was commissioned to direct an improv format that someone else had created. The show idea he had was to take an obituary from that day's *New York Times* and improvise a longform that explored that person's life. The challenge was in figuring out how to adapt a story with very specific details (childhood info, accomplishments, etc.) derived from a public source and following the arc without overcomplicating the structure of the piece.

The first task as a director was to find where the focus of the show was, regardless of who the subject was. I researched various obituaries to see what types of stories would appear in that section. There were influential figures from the arts, scientists who solved a particular medical mystery, lawyers and activists who led a certain cause. The stories were all varied but all shared the fact that they were rather dramatic tales of a person who rose to the top of their field. In most cases, there was a specific event that especially brought that individual notice.

From this I started making notes with decisions that I could build from or stray from:

1. *The obituary needs to be selected ahead of time.* Because there is such specific information that will be part of the story, in some cases

involving a specific culture or field, we want to give the actors a chance to research. Otherwise their lack of knowledge will be glaringly apparent since the audience will have the source material to compare it to. This will in turn make the players hesitant in making choices. I made the decision to notify the cast in the morning when the paper came out and gave them certain related topics that we would want to research to fill out the improv.

2. *The story needs to be cast.* The specifics of any story varied based on the size of the piece but most were plentiful with details. The responsibility of carrying all that knowledge into any show was too much of a burden for any one performer. For instance, one show followed the life of a Vietnamese dissident who was active in the revolution prior to the Vietnam War. There was a large amount of cultural information as well as historical data that would be relevant. Casting people into specific roles would help divvy up those duties while others would be cast under general headings. Letting some actors know they would play various friends and family of the dissident helped them focus on cultural information. Other actors were assigned to play authority figures and work relations, thus setting them to focus on more historical information. Casting the lead, the subject of the obituary, helped guarantee that the role was taken on definitively and immediately making it clear to the audience. I decided it was not something that I wanted to leave to chance in the improvisation. Also, it allowed me to match the personality of the character with the appropriate actor. Some actors did better with more rigid characters, some with more emotionally complicated characters.

3. *The piece would need to be freeform.* There would be a huge obligation to get the story right for the actors. Going through it chronologically would only put more pressure on them to hit certain landmarks in the subject's life, allowing themselves to get panicked if they hit events too soon or if events were missed altogether. A freeform structure would allow them to play out the details that held the most resonance with them and could then get behind most. Any details that were "missed" could easily be gotten to with a time

jump or represented in a parallel scene: a newscast, the view of an average citizen influenced by the events, etc. Furthermore, they could jump off on occasional tangents when they felt particularly bogged down with the content.

4. _There would need to be a relationship focus._ If we go too freeform with tangents there is a chance of spinning out of control unless we have a focus we can return too. A central relationship would give the actors something that can be revisited and built throughout the arc. To do this we would cast a player in a specific secondary character role. This player, as well as the one who was playing the lead would not be able to play any other roles, so as to make sure the audience and the rest of the troupe would not get confused. The secondary role would not have to be a protagonist per se, since the conflict could come from an outside source (a political event, a national tragedy, a scientific enigma to be solved) as long as the character presented at least the slightest variation on perspective. The secondary characters ranged from professional rivals to spouses who would stick with them through the rough times.

With these decisions in place I could start to plan out the rehearsal schedule regardless of whether or not these would eventually be part of the piece. I knew I had enough time for mistakes to be made while still having the troupe prepared for opening night.

CHAPTER 8: DIRECTING WITH TECH AND MUSIC

How do you relate to the person you have sitting in the lighting booth or the person at the piano during the show? Do you consider them to be another *player* in the troupe or a completely different *layer* of the show that can be looked at separately?

Do you have a lighting person or a technical director? Do you have a musician/accompanist or a musical director? A lighting person (player) makes offers like spotlighting a monologue and general editing calls but does not make artistic decisions on the lighting setup. A technical director (layer) assesses the best lighting coverage and makes decisions on the overall "look" of the show. Similarly a musician/accompanist (player) is a strictly functional component who doesn't always come to rehearsals—sometimes they even just show up for the shows—while a musical director (layer) leads vocal warm-ups and makes choices toward how the music is represented in the show.

> As an ensemble member, a musician should be part of regular rehearsals, and be given the same chance as the performers to experiment, risk, and become attuned to everyone involved.
>
> —*Michael Pollock*

Differentiating between layer and player will help you know better how to facilitate and direct your musical and technical person. What parameters do you set for their involvement in the troupe? How much artistic input do you allow them? Do they initiate offers or are you looking for them to strictly enhance what the players onstage are doing? If they are to initiate, does that include edits, entrances and heightening in a scene?

I made a decision long ago to stop working with musicians and to start working with musical directors. This is more than just semantics. It meant that I needed to delegate a huge chunk of the project to someone who I am empowering to lead, creating a stronger dynamic for communicating in areas that I was not strong. In the superhero show, Ka-Baam!!, our musical director was Travis Ploeger who oversaw all vocal warm-ups and the general tone of the show, freeing me up to focus on other facets of the show.

Empowering your lighting person to be a technical director and your musician to be your musical director will invest them further in the process and, if they are experienced enough, will open up your production in new directions that you might not have forseen.

Of course, if they are available for such a commitment, you may need to perceive them as players. This means that you set specific parameters with them on what their position involves. Many musicians and lighting people that I have seen are paid for their time (even while the performers are not) and there is a reason for that. It clarifies and simplifies the relationship.

However, they should be involved in that decision. There are people who wish to be more involved with the troupe with which they are working, or to at least wish to have that option presented to them.

IMPROV LIGHTING TECHNIQUE

For any improv show I direct, I always do the lights. It keeps me involved, it keeps me with a certain modicum of control, and quite frankly, it keeps me aware of everything going on on the stage so I can take appropriate notes. It's too easy to get caught up in the entertainment value of something when you're just an audience member, a director sitting in the audience for the show. I like to be really involved as a performer and I think tech is as involved as any other role.

—*Don Hall*

Just as actors have the tools of character, status and emotion to use in their work, the lighting improviser also has an extensive array of choices to pull from. Your lighting person can help the scenes by highlighting mood or casting added significance upon a moment. Understanding these choices will help you better communicate your concepts to them. Not everyone has access to full lightboards with pre-set dimmer boards and multiple rows of lights and gels. Some of you are doing shows in a room at the Student Union or the backroom of a bar with nothing more than an on/off switch. So let's look at a lighting person's tools, starting with the simplest setup to the most sophisticated. Remember, this is no substitute for a professional text on theater lighting. It is merely a starting point to help you begin an understanding of the possibilities.

Timing—I have seen the lighting in a scene get a huge laugh just based on when they came down. The decision of what is seen and what isn't is the most basic of the control that the tech has. It goes beyond just finding the end of a scene (also called a *button*) with a blackout, which is a huge skill. It is also knowing when to cut the lights to enhance the action. If a killer is coming up on his victim with a knife, or a lover is moving in for a kiss, the action is made stronger based on where the lights are cut. A good connection with the lighting person can open up opportunities like this within the scene rather than just the end, allowing for a time jump or furthering the action. What does it look like if we go to black before the killer connects with the knife or the lovers' lips touch?

Imagine a killer is approaching unbeknownst to the victim when the lights black out. When they come up again, the victim is down on the floor with the killer standing above him crying. Why is he crying? We don't know yet but with the help of the lighting person we were able to jump to a less obvious choice more easily. Now, imagine the characters switching places during the blackout with the victim crying over the killer's dead body.

Brightness—The next level of sophistication is having dimmer control. The intensity of the lighting is an easy way for the tech to establish mood such as putting the lights very low for a horror genre scene. If you have nothing more than general room lighting with a single, round dimmer switch, you can make your options broader by creating a box around the switch with masking tape. Then, with a marker, you can make notches showing where you can turn the dial to for different levels of lighting, the most important of which is what the minimum amount of light is by which the actors can still see.

Isolations—If there are multiple lights in the space you are using, you can establish what are called *isolations*. These are lights devoted to covering specific areas of the stage (such as a center spotlight). When the lighting instruments are all brought up, they give coverage of the entire stage, or a *wash*. A lighting director can heighten focus on an action on the stage by isolating it in a spotlight, putting the rest of the tableau in darkness. Having a tight spotlight will affect the mood of a monologue, making it seem sinister or claustrophobic. Dividing up the stage through the arrangement of lights also increases the theatricality of the performance by creating a lighting vocabulary (e.g. the center light is the emcee light, a division down the middle of the stage for a split screen, monologues can be delivered in the downstage right spotlight, etc.). Many instruments also have *shutters*, flaps or screens that can be moved to decrease the size of the spot.

Transition and sequence—If there are isolations, you can also play with transitioning between lights or activating them in sequence for new effects. Imagine we have a scene between two love interests who have yet to share how they feel about each other. The scene shows them talking around it until they get to a point where they cannot hold it back any longer and they both move in for a kiss. The lighting person, seeing this buildup, transitions to a spotlight to keep the players close to each other and then, when they make contact in the kiss, brings up a full, bright wash, showing how their world has changed. Going from the use of one light to another or to the use of many lights is a tool that a lighting person can use to signify any dynamic change.

Color and shape—Many theaters have a catalog of *gels*, colored sheets of plastic that are laid over the rim of the lighting instrument. Colored gels are the easiest way for a lighting person to contribute to the mood or environment of the theater piece. A blue wash suggests a night scene. Red gives a sinister undertone, or, when blinked on and off, invokes a motel vacancy sign. Most theatre lights have a frame that holds the gels in place which can also be used to affix a *gobo*. A gobo is a cut pattern that when light shines through it, creates a lighting effect on stage. For instance a round cover with slits cut into it can throw the light to look as if it is shining through venetian blinds. Gobos can be bought (though they can easily be made by cutting into thick card stock) that simulate cloud cover, a canopy of branches, or an array of abstract patterns.

Direction—The more lighting instruments you have, the more isolations you can create. With this you can also play with the direction of light. Most improv setups focus on providing a strong amount of front light for maximum coverage during a show. If you have the equipment, play with backlighting to employ a new palette of moods. For more stylized shows, you can set up lights at the wings of the stage to create more dynamic entrances.

Movement—Some theaters are blessed with a lighting package that includes a travelling spot that can be shifted at any point of the show to throw an isolation on any part of the stage, including areas in the audience. In addition to the bonus of adaptability, a new vocabulary of options comes with movement. Rolling the light around a dark stage can simulate a prison spotlight. Panning the light across the stage in a straight horizontal line can give the impression of headlights in the distance.

As we can see, lighting has many possibilities—comparable to the infinite number of choices available to any of the players on stage. Lighting can emphasize a significant moment or action, create patterns that help develop a character or environment, and not just help find the ends of scenes.

THE MUSICAL LAYER

Music has even more complexities than lights. The average troupe employs a keyboardist to accompany them; that is eighty-eight individual instruments that can be used in limitless combinations. Add to that the options that are added by the use of a sustain pedal, volume, and a keyboard's programming that allows it to mimic up to a hundred different instruments and you can see why. A good place for your research to start would be either of the books that Michael Pollock has written on the art of musical improv and musical improv accompaniment to give you a solid foundation before delving into books on music theory. Meanwhile, we will focus on how to communicate with a musical collaborator when you have a minimal knowledge of music.

I myself have only the most basic ideas about music, mixed with remnants of the occasional advanced lesson: pitch, tempo, singing the tonic note, etc. I can never hope to know as much as any musician and this has gotten in the way of my directing them. The production value added by the inclusion of music, however, was too valuable to lose. So you learn to reference.

> Let the keyboard player translate your thoughts into musical expression. We've all seen every kind of musical underscore there is extensively on TV and film. Use associations like soap operas, romantic comedies, sitcoms, awards shows, dramas, animated features, to communicate the brand of accompaniment you're thinking of. If the musician you're working with has the sort of observant knack for this that you require, he or she will connect easily with that kind of guidance.
>
> —*Michael Pollock*

Any good direction begins with a strong starting point. Finding the common frame of reference as suggested in the quote above, even it if does not match your vision exactly, is a fantastic place to build from. Then, similarly to the way a sculptor takes away from the slab of marble until the figure emerges from it, you can take away what does match the feeling of your idea from the set piece of music. Earlier, we discussed pulling scenes from movies to create templates for improvisation, and now are making intensely specific musical choices to create a foundation for your musician to pull from.

> The artistic director should speak in terms of desired effects. It's not necessary to use musical terms, really—just discuss the desired result.
>
> —*Michael Pollock*

The key thing is to have an opinion, some idea or starting point from which the musician can build. Not all musicians are thrilled with the direction of "play anything." In fact, for some it can be frustrating, especially because it draws out the process of discovering what it is you need.

> Although this lack of direction might simply mean that the director trusts the accompanist enough to play appropriate music consistent with the rules and style of the troupe, it makes it difficult for the entire troupe to evolve together (if the musician is a member of the troupe), or to play together comfortably (even if he or she isn't a member).
>
> —*Jamey Rosen*

Here are some areas to consider when looking at the inclusion of music in your improvisation:

Reference—How much do you want the musician to reference known music? Pulling in specific pieces of music can ground a piece or make it gaggy. Avoiding them can allow for a more freeform feel or can make the piece too vague.

Continuity—How often do you want the music to be a part of scenes? Some formats are assisted by having just the transitions underscored while certain genres require a more constant musical presence.

Textural vs. Melodic—Should the musician focus on making musical offers to be more dominated by changes in mode, style, and tone, and melodic themes that can be used to progress the action, make offers with callbacks to melodies already established, etc.? Or should the musician be more textural, creating a vocabulary of sounds where musical offers tend to be dominated by changes in rhythm and volume? Melodic accompaniment tends to be more subtle and continuous while textural accompaniment tends to be more obvious and offers are separated by long silences. A continuum exists between these two methods, but as a director you might have a strong preference.

Spotlighting—An important musicial contribution, similar to lighting, is in how it can add emphasis, to a moment or an entrance, as we will see when we look at the arc of the scene. Are there specific facts the musician should focus on more? Less?

I can only show you so much, as I only know so much, but you should have a good place to begin a discussion with your musician on how to proceed. Ultimately, he is the best person to define the terms of the music and is more than willing to share it with you. Learn that from them and then make some choices. Allow yourself room in the process to make some wrong choices. Anywhere you start is valid.

THE SCENIC ARC

Every scene has an arc and the audience is following it. Your tech person needs to develop their eye for spotting that arc and prepare ahead of time for the button (the line or action that caps the scene). Meanwhile, the musician needs to explore how and when to enter the scene and support the emotional base or mood of the scene. How do we train them for that? The Extend/Continue exercise that we used for sidecoaching is also a good tool for learning what their tendencies are. Are they calling for emotional extensions? Are they calling for extensions on the activity? One is not more preferred than the other, but focusing too much on activity will distract them from noticing the emotional build of the scene. The activity helps ground the scene with narrative but it can be followed too closely as if it is what the scene is truly about. Some scenes need to return to that activity before resolving the scene to give it a context for the audience. In the movie *Throw Momma from the Train*, we need to see Billy Crystal's character return to his typewriter and begin writing for his character to come full circle, even though we have seen him hit his emotional peak.

An arc can take many shapes though many will try to create the rule of when to pull the lights, the most popular being to pull on a big laugh or closing line. There are benefits to purposefully cutting an arc in different ways. In horror movies, there are times that you see the kill, times when you pull away just before the axe comes down, times when all you see is the shadow of the approaching villain. Each choice presents the narrative differently even though we know that the same result will occur—our character is going to end up dead.

Allow your troupe to experiment on different cutaways. For example, give your actors scenarios that revolve around a central action: lovers getting their first kiss, a baseball player up at bat in the final out of the final inning, a prisoner seeing a chance for escape. Have them play a simple quick scene, something that can easily be repeated. Now, in repeating the scene, have the tech person pull the lights at different points in the scene to convey to a time jump and see how the actors use the offer.

You should train your actors to roll with the unexpected, something that is expected in working improvisationally. Players are too often compelled to point out when a lighting person cuts the lights too early or lets a scene go too long. This feels valid as an argument, but not when you are supposed to be yes-anding *all* offers onstage. That includes those of the technical director.

These unexpected technical choices can be huge opportunities rather than mistakes. Cutting the lights early on in a scene creates a chance for time jumps, replays or interstitial scenes. Imagine this scenario where the lights were cut at a point in the scene that doesn't make immediate sense: Characters A and B are talking about A's upcoming date, clearly defining a third character. As the scene progresses, B leaves the scene, expecting another player to jump into the role of the aforementioned date, but no one ever does, leaving A waiting. The lighting person thinking the scene is going nowhere, takes out the lights. What if:

a. When the lights come back up A is still waiting but the stage picture is slightly modified to show a passage of time. The actor could be engaged in an activity while waiting, or even slumped over to show an increase in age.

b. The lights come back up and Character A immediately initiates the same scene with B. A could modify the details showing he is going to be equally disappointed but now with a different date. A could keep the details the same but change his persona. If in the first scene he said, "This date is going to be great," he could play with having more of a blasé attitude about it this time.

    c.   The lights come back up on A's date stuck in traffic, off with someone else, walking on the moon, etc.

A common issue in training a new technical person is when they follow the action too closely. There have been many times when the guy in the booth would initiate a blackout on a scene with a gradual fade of the lights, only to bump them back up at the slightest hint of a new offer. The audience sees this transition in progress even if the actors do not and they see the error made in taking them back to full. Train your tech person to be decisive and bold in his choices. It adds stronger production value to the final product than having someone who does the job without confidence.

CHAPTER 9: BEING A DIRECTOR AND PERFORMER

> You cannot choose to direct the group because no one else will direct it. You have to choose to direct the group because you want to and you have to be the kind of personality that can deal with the fact that you're not always going to be everybody's buddy.
>
> —*Mark Sutton*

Sometimes the concept behind a custom-made project is so personal that you cannot help but be involved on both a directing and performing level. Those of you in smaller improv communities have no choice but to wear both a director's and performer's hat simultaneously. In doing so, you are running into more issues than those who have avoided that overlap. The easier dynamic is to not do both, or to at least allow the project to develop some momentum of its own before entering as a performer. Even then, there are complications that come from doing the double duty. The primary concern is in distinguishing between the two jobs so that they don't bleed over and overcomplicate an already complicated situation.

There is a reason why this chapter is one of the shortest in the book. Many of the directors that I spoke with avoid performing with the troupe they are directing. This is what their years of experience have shown them. There are good reasons for this and there are few safeguards that can be offered. For those of you who are limited in options or gluttons for punishment, here are some things to consider.

WHICH HAT WHEN?

When you are in charge of a group of people, it is hard to let that leadership role go, but this is what you need to do when you are performing with them. I have seen many instances where the director becomes the most ubiquitous player, popping up in more scenes than necessary to "fix" them. Rather than playing from their instincts, they are playing from their knowledge. Rather than attacking a scene organically, they are attacking it surgically. They have trouble concentrating on just being a performer and end up being an outsider in the improvisation.

This is tiring to keep up. An improv scene is a shared responsibility and when you take it upon yourself to fill in everyone else's gaps, you are doing more than your share. Furthermore, it is intrusive. Players can become irritated when they are not given a chance to participate.

Good directors do not direct from within the show. If you were in the audience, watching the performance with your notebook, you wouldn't suddenly jump onstage to fix something. You need to show the same restraint when you are performing. You cannot fix the show from inside. You need to trust that the cast is strong enough and let the show be what it's going to be. This is that margin of error I commented on early on in this book. It is a necessary evil of improvising.

This is why you need to give every rehearsal a chance before you interrupt with a performer's hat on. Taking your turn in scenework when certain ideas are still being absorbed by your troupe will work against it. Let exercises develop their own momentum before you try it. It will look like a compliment in that you want in on the fun that the others are having. Your participation as a performer should be the afterthought. You need to sacrifice your own progress rather than that of the show. The group will feel more taken care of and will be able to better take care of you when it's your turn.

When that time comes, check yourself before getting out on stage with your group. All performers need to have a bit of the director in them, particularly when it comes to editing scenes, but it requires an equal balance with the parts that are writers and actors. As we discussed in the chapter on notes, issues are best avoided when we are distracted from them. When you are one of the performers starting a scene, make a strong choice that you can hold on to. Your best bet is to focus on emotionally- or character-based choices that will affect your perspective enough that you will stay in the moment.

If you find yourself entering scenes and overtaking them, then you need to shorten your stay. Quicker appearances will limit how much you allow yourself to add and gives your players a chance to build on their own. Sometimes, however, that stage can be like quicksand and once you step out into it, you find yourself stuck and sinking in further. It helps to make the choice to add from outside rather than inside whenever possible. Soundtracking a scene to help the moment, adding a special effect, or calling a narrative cue (such as "later that day" or "meanwhile, elsewhere") are good ways to offer a scene a push while still keeping a distance. It becomes an extension of your sidecoaching. Once you experience this mindset often enough, you will find it easier to do scenic entrances and exits quickly without overstaying your welcome.

Some directors get thrown in the opposite direction—that of hanging back and not directly participating for fear of overstepping their bounds and not giving other players a chance. There is only so much responsibility you can take for other people's stage time. Making a choice to not do something out of fear is not a healthy way of thinking for any player, particularly a director. If this becomes the case, try some initiative challenges where you focus on endowing those around you in the scene. This will help you to be more involved in the action without guilt.

GETTING AND GIVING NOTES

Many inexperienced directors who I have seen perform suffer from what I call "director's disease." Without anyone to look after them and guide them, their performance skills tend to suffer. It is difficult to grow artistically without any outside direction. Applying challenges to distract yourself from being a director is only part of the solution. Because improvisation is such a personal artform, sometimes the thing that needs the most work can remain hidden when looked at from the inside.

If you don't have someone from outside the troupe who can give their observations, then you need to rely on the eye of your teammates to guide you. Without it, you will often find yourself plateauing with no direction to explore and nothing to challenge you. To accomplish this, ego-free, you need to create an environment as clear of judgment as possible, as you attempt to be simultaneously on the same level with the other players and in charge of them.

Notes are already personal. The added task of noting from within a show works against the noting process while causing personal issues to enter the group dynamic if the right vocabulary is not in place. When looking at a show, it can be enough to ask the group which scene was the most fun to perform, where the show felt the strongest, and what can be explored further. These terms are devoid of using words like "good" or "bad" as a way of creating a more level field for discussion. This helps cap the bitterness that can creep in. In extreme cases, there will be players who will question notes from a director who has performance flaws of her own. Some will retaliate against poor notes with their own if given the chance. Both of these reactions are obviously counterproductive. Creating a routine after each show, where you ask about specific show aspects without going into too much detail, is the first step in steering clear of this.

Just as with exercises and how they can be strictly structured to maintain focus, setting a structure with an exact vocabulary can set a tone of professionalism. The best format is listing where the show was strongest and what areas will be explored next rehearsal or performance. Have a time limit and repeat key observations made by others to both regain the focus and control of the discussion and help prioritize the notes. At the end of the allotted time, repeat the key things that were said.

> Any chance I can, I play with [my team] which a lot of coaches and teachers will go, "What the hell are you doing? That's a conflict of interest!" And then I give them notes afterwards, "Please, support me more." Actually, because we now discuss the notes and we point out where we made mistakes and I don't hammer them, and if they can't figure out where the mistake was made I can help them figure it out, we still do it in shows that I perform in. We did a show here last night and we talked about it afterwards and I said, "You know, I probably made a mistake when I came back in, I probably should've left it out," and we talked about it for a little while.
>
> —*Jeff Griggs*

The second step is getting and giving individual notes. This might be done best one-on-one. Getting notes from a performer or two on the side will eliminate the intentions that are sometimes perceived as vendettas when done in front of a group. Specifically, I am talking about the want of a performer who wants to knock you off of your high horse with a critique that may not be all that constructive. Similarly, performers will look at certain notes as being "inappropriate" in front of others and will question their validity as a result. Always remember that another option is to let certain notes go in favor of another, more helpful focus.

> Sometimes it is enough to know you are right and keep it to yourself.
>
> —*Jill Bernard*

This is all part of the ridiculous politics that are present in any group, but with the right vocabulary in place you can minimize the stress and chaos of the situation.

If possible, find someone to fill the role of assistant director in the group, to help create a system of checks and balances. This will be someone who can play the role of observer when you need to switch hats or to help divvy up the directorial responsibilities. For instance, while viewing a practice set, you could have the assistant director watch certain performers to see if they perform on their overall patterns while you watch the group as a whole.

This creates a different dynamic in that we are delegating some responsibility which empowers whomever is in that role. This responsibility can be spread universally throughout the group in rehearsal in smaller ways as well by assigning players to do such things as calling the blackouts. Through doing this you can put your focus elsewhere, while training the other players to be stronger observers. This will only help their improv work improve.

CHAPTER 10: DEALING WITH ISSUES WITHIN A GROUP

> If someone comes to you and reveals something that is hurting them, because it's blocking them onstage, it is my job as a director to help them get past that, but not get through it. Or to go around it. It is not my job to play therapist in a rehearsal process. So, there's a line between being a cultural anthropologist in their world and being their therapist.
>
> —*Michael Gellman*

If you have pursued directing then it is for a love of the artform or a want to lead or because of an all-consuming vision. You take pride in your leadership, your skill, your lessons. You get a thrill from being a director. What you probably don't enjoy, however, is being a den mother. Unfortunately, this is an unavoidable side effect of working intimately with the collaboration of personalities that make up any improv troupe. Politics arise anytime more than one person is involved in a project and grow more so with each person added. At any given time you may have to play the role of the father figure, the confidante or the disciplinarian.

If you were hoping to find answers in this chapter that directly solve what your group is dealing with, then you are going to walk away unsatisfied. What you will find, hopefully, are some guidelines that may help make dealing with problems easier.

The general maintenance of your troupe is an ongoing mental challenge; with luck, your improvisational skills can be applied to areas outside the stage.

Rule #1: Establish ground rules, often.

In an improv scene, the reality is established by what is spoken, and nothing can be assumed unless stated; the same goes for the group dynamic. Certain details get set immediately in any group or project: when rehearsals are going to be, how many shows, whether people are going to get paid or need to pitch in. As the process goes on, other details are developed: casting for the shows, dress code, lateness policy. It is impossible to plan for every contingency that will come up, but you can learn to roll with the punches by setting ground rules and reiterating as needed.

Rule #2: Deal with the consequences, not the causes.

Acting is a series of actions and reactions. In a scene, if we focus too much on the other person's actions, rather than developing our reactions, we stifle the flow. Similarly, in interpersonal relationships, there is the pitfall of getting too caught up in the details of why something happened rather than its effects. It seems perfectly logical to want to resolve the why, but when you are dealing with a situation like having two cast members who are dating and having problems that are bleeding into rehearsals, then trust me, you don't want to know why. You just want to prevent it from causing damage to the troupe. The best way to not get involved in the personal issues is to not get yourself involved.

Rule #3: The group trumps the individual.

No one person is more valuable than the entire troupe. That is the case in the improvisation and that is the case in the group dynamic. I have seen some players placed on pedestals by their directors, sometimes bending over backwards for the player, making far more allowances than makes sense. I realize there are great players who we do not want to lose, but we need to consider the tradeoff that might affect the quality of the group as a whole.

Rule #4: State the goals for both sides to achieve.

Eight times out of ten, when an issue needs to be addressed with a player, they are fully aware of the issue. Sometimes, they are even dying to have it dealt with and breathe a sigh of relief when I bring it up. Similarly to Rule #2, it is helpful to be forward thinking, focusing on what you need from the individual rather than the problems you have gotten from them thus far.

Rule #5: Assign responsibility.

Life, like improv, comprises choices and commitments. Any decision that is made needs to be committed to. When issues are addressed with a player, you want to get a sense of what they are willing to be responsible for in the coming rehearsals. The one who is often tardy will commit to a certain change in behavior. It might be rearranging other aspects of their life to make it on time. It might just be giving you a better sense from week to week as to when you can expect them. You and the player both need to be realistic. It is so easy to promise something that will never be followed through on. While you are in negotiations on how to resolve the issue, remove consequences from the table—this will reduce the player's hesitancy to offer solutions that might not be in your best interest. Incomplete ideas can spawn stronger ideas. For instance, a player who is consitently late finally admits that she cannot make it on time because of personal issues, and offers to be at rehearsals no more than half an hour late and to get notes from her colleagues. You can take this as a start and by mixing and matching its elements with your own ideas, find a realistic compromise.

Rule #6: Learn to adapt.
These are not rules so much as training wheels. They are subject to change based on the particulars of your relationship with your troupe and how it grows.

DEALING WITH LATENESSES

> If you don't have that discipline, then everyone's going to start letting go a little bit. Not because they're jerks or because they don't care but because it's just the tendency. People will start to show up late and it's like, no. Even though this may be a show where you're not getting paid or you're not going to really do it in front of a lot of people or you're just going to do it in front of other students, you've got to be able to instill that idea of if you were in a play in college or if you were on a TV show you have to start behaving in that way, the professional way.
>
> *—Armando Diaz*

Lateness is the most common issue that comes up in the course of rehearsals. Things happen; it is inevitable. What you need to focus on is minimizing the effect of latenesses on the rehearsal process. My personal issue is having to repeat myself at the top of the session so I wait to allow everyone to get there before beginning. But how do you know when people will be arriving? My tactic is this: I do not care about whether players are late as much as I care about knowing how late they will be. I set a policy with my cast that at the top of every session I will be checking my voice mail. If people know they are going to be late, they should leave a message estimating how late. Even if they have to make themselves later by getting off the subway to make that phone call, it is still better to have a player be thirty minutes late and know it, than have them be fifteen minutes late and not know. Once I have that information, I can make a better judgment of whether to begin warm-ups, wait for additional people, or reorganize the beginning exercises. Some warm-ups have a quorum of people necessary to conduct them properly, and if there are not enough people, the plan gets thrown. You learn to adapt to situations on those occasions by switching the order, doing something unplanned or experimental. I like to lead one-minute scenes to get people working together while we wait for others so that no time is wasted.

When I am teaching a workshop and lateness occurs, the pressure to discipline is gone, but the pressure to be all-inclusive is higher. I try to make the time waiting for latecomers proportional to the percentage of the class missing. There is no formula that you can write out; it is just something that you feel out for yourself. In the end, this time is on the dime of those attending and you want them all to get their money's worth. You will know what the cutoff is between allowing for those paying customers who have yet to arrive to get the most out of the class and those paying customers who are being made to wait. At that point the responsibility shifts from your shoulders onto those of the latecomers.

Recurring lateness is a different issue. Whenever any issue becomes more regular it is a sign of something deeper. At this time, you need to organize your priorities and boundaries.

Why is it important that they come to rehearsal on time? So that the performers don't miss any new developments in the work. Why is that necessary? So that the performers can be more prepared for the show. What happens if the performers are not prepared? They are not able to put on the best possible performance.

This is where we find our main concern. Therefore, based on the above train of thought, someone who is continually late or absent should be pulled from shows. If the problem persists, then obviously the work that the group is doing has fallen as a priority for them. Are you willing to work with people who feel this way?

Don't think it is necessarily easier when you are able to pay the performers. We have all goofed off on the job in some capacity. There will equally be someone who will goof off in the group.

Make sure that when you ask yourself the string of questions above, that you are as objective and honest as you can be. For instance, a group that is rehearsing regularly without performances might need to scale back on rehearsals. A group where the better players are taking advantage with their lateness might need to have rehearsals devoted to helping those struggling to improve. That judgment call is completely up to you and your sensibilities.

DEALING WITH UNPROFESSIONALISM

Lateness is one example of how troupe members work below the necessary requirements. While you are investing a lot of energy, the others are not showing as much commitment. They do not see the harm in missing a rehearsal or arriving at a less than full capacity, sometimes with a meal in hand that they had to pick up prior and have to eat now. Perhaps they enjoy grabbing focus from you while you are leading with a joke or side note that shows how brilliant they are. The demon of unprofessionalism may manifest itself in different ways but the roots tend to look the same.

Create a mission statement with your group. You can do it verbally but it always helps to have a more tangible version. Build it with the group and make sure that it is one that everybody can agree with. This is a good way to keep yourself in check. We directors have all had our moments of fanaticism where vision of some artistic utopia prevents us from being fully realistic.

As a result we opt for more rehearsal time, enthusiastically push for people to give the project focus on their own time and generally forget that most people who get involved in improvisation do so for the fun of it. When you create a schedule, factor in people's availabilities, the number of members, and the number of performances slated. Any other factors might be a side result of your otherwise productive enthusiasm. The last thing you want is for your troupe to burn out before the show comes around.

If by all objective standards, however, your scheduling is perfectly sane, then we can discuss the specific member's reactions. Most disagreements about what is required of membership comes from it having not been thoroughly discussed. Many improvisers assume that their priorities are shared with those around them. Not only is this not reasonable, it can prove to be destructive.

There is an unspoken compact made within any group that is discovered only in times of conflict. You want to preempt any chance for confusion as to what you need to properly direct the group. Do not assume any aspect is above mentioning, or even mentioning more than once. Similarly, you want your players to be very clear about what their commitments are. How many hours a week are they committed to rehearsing? What other duties are they willing to take on? Give your group a chance to get together just to compare lists of what are acceptable parameters for the project you are working on together.

DEALING WITH BURNOUT OR STAGNATION

As the saying goes, it is possible to have too much of a good thing. In the case of performing and rehearsing, this means getting to a point of burnout, where one loses energy for the work, or stagnation, where there is no lack of energy but no discernable growth over a long period of time. These are two situations that are tough to face from inside the problem. A performer needs to be made aware of the new pattern that has arisen and given a focus that will help combat it. In more extreme situations, a person needs to change their overall habits.

Burnout or stagnation usually comes as a result of over-saturation. Even something as fun as performing can feel like a chore if the routine of it is repeated often enough. The best solution is for the players to take a break from the work, give themselves some space and to come back, hopefully, with a new appreciation for being part of the group. In a tighter schedule, this may be impossible. How else can you change that person's environment so that they are able to play again? Perhaps you can change their role, put them in control of edits while not being in the piece. Anything that alters their perspective or relationship with what their brain perceives as the norm will make it easier for that player to change their burnout pattern.

The burnout can also be a side effect of that improviser being overburdened, in which case, a new contract needs to be made. They may need to pare down their schedule to what makes more sense emotionally, either with outside projects or within the troupe. The idea of losing a player part-time may seem horrible, but if there is too much going on in their head, they are not really there anyway. Allowing them room to reevaluate will make their time with you, while lessened, stronger.

DEALING WITH INTERPERSONAL PROBLEMS

Troupes get close socially—that is unavoidable. You're learning each other's instincts, getting to a point where you are finishing each other's thoughts; it can feel very intimate. It is completely understandable that this occasionally evolves into romantic relationships. While it is not the best choice to date within the group, there is no point in getting in the way of it.

> Whoever is fucking whom is none of my business...whatever is happening with them in their personal lives, with their love lives, with their finances, with their romances. I don't need to know their god or their spirituality, unless they want to share it. There are aspects of their lives that I don't need, that are none of my business.
>
> —*Michael Gellman*

I was performing in an ensemble improv show that a friend of mine was directing when two of the other cast members secretly began dating. I was aware of it because I am a close friend of one half of the couple. The director had a hunch this was going on (as did some of the other players, I'll bet) and started noticing behavioral problems. The two of them were at times disruptive, or were being weird with each other.

Determined to nip this in the bud, my director friend confronted the two as to whether or not they were a couple. They denied it each time it was addressed. He grew more frustrated as the season continued, the situation did not improve, and their relationship became more obvious. Even though he had enjoyed working with both the performers and found they had contributed greatly to the project, he was soured on the idea of ever working with them again.

As a director, he was great, except for drawing boundaries between personal issues and professional ones. There is no doubt that the disruptions needed to be addressed firmly and stopped. But the reasons behind them are irrelevant most of the time. The same goes for two players who are fighting.

Pull the two players aside and state clearly and matter-of-factly what you are seeing in objective terms and what their consequences are. "I have been noticing some tension in these side conversations that have been going on and it is making me lose track of the rehearsal." Do not allow for debate on what you are seeing while allowing yourself to be wrong. "I might be misreading things but just in case I am not, I wanted to put a stop to it." Depending on how confident you feel in your observations, you can follow up with an ultimatum that clearly puts responsibility on them, once again without getting involved in the back story. "I would hate to lose either of you but I may have no choice if these disruptions continue."

DEALING WITH MEMBERS' PERSONAL PROBLEMS

As I mentioned earlier, it is best to not get involved in the specifics of the why, but with personal issues that line is not always so clear. People bring in baggage all the time, ranging dramatically in intensity: break-ups, work troubles, death in the family, etc. Your personality sets its own boundaries on how deeply you will relate with the rest of a troupe on a personal level. There is no mandatory distance, but you do need to assess what that relationship is before you delve into a member's personal problems. Your dynamic of keeping a professional distance from the other members might require for you to establish a liaison—someone who you recognize is close to the person who is troubled and can help them with their issues—who you can discuss the situation with on a more technical level. Quarantine the two from the rest of rehearsal and keep the rest of the troupe on the improvisation. Chances are that others noticed the one member was going through something emotional and you want to establish a tone that none of this is a big deal.

Hopefully, the liaison helps the issue enough that rehearsal can resume for everyone, but nothing is guaranteed. Your next step needs to be to create space for that person to get through their issue. This is where the why becomes relevant as you will have to make a judgment call as to what warrants taking time away. Some personal problems need to be pushed through, particularly the residue of an earlier argument, while life-altering events like a breakup or death need to be given time and space.

In such cases, you want to make a new contract with that member. I would give them the rehearsal off, relieving them of the responsibility of maintaining this relationship right now and establishing with them a timeframe of when they might return, or you might check in with them about returning. Depending on the situation, you might want to call on a liaison again if this might be too awkward for both parties, considering your relationship.

It is possible to overburden the liaison or overinflate her importance if you are not precise about the parameters of what you need. Establish what you need from the distraught player. What is the new contract? Is the player excused from rehearsal until a later time or date? Say something along the lines of, "I would like for him to be able to participate in tonight's rehearsal. Please see how much time he needs to himself before he can rejoin us. If he needs more than an hour, I suggest that he go home and contact me about the next rehearsal." You can be as clinical or cold as you need to be to communicate your wants and let the liaison present it in a way that is more sensitive.

DEALING WITH INTERNAL CRITIQUES & DISCONTENT

> I was trying to be delicate and I think maybe that was the wrong thing to do.
> The idea is to not worry about their egos and to make sure that they work as part of the group.
>
> —*Kevin Patrick Robbins*

Egos are one of the biggest obstacles in working with a group. Some people have a problem relinquishing complete control during the process and can wreak havoc on a rehearsal with side comments or outward defiance. It is tough to keep one's anger in check during all this. Discontent is an energy just like happiness or fear. It is real and tangible and cannot just be eliminated; it needs to be diverted. You can create outlets for discontent to make it less destructive and more constructive.

The first step is creating a regular forum for members' thoughts. Directors who have auditioned their cast for a project need not set this up but ensembles with ongoing rehearsals and shows could use this structure to alleviate the strain. A forum can range from regularly asking "What are your thoughts from inside that scene?" to setting up a rehearsal devoted to discussion. The most severe damage to a group can come from what is left unsaid or, even worse, said to the wrong parties. Animosity festers underneath, affecting how the players interact; if they release it to a particular comrade either inside or outside the group, it creates little mutinies. Let people get it out under your supervision. It will be healthier for everyone involved.

For extreme cases of general discontent within the group, there is the withhold circle which my friend Matt Dominianni introduced to our college group. The procedure is as follows: Everyone sits in a circle. One person addresses someone else in the circle with "Name, there is something I've withheld from you." That person then responds with "Okay, would you like to tell me?" The first person then says whatever they need to—it can be positive or negative. During this whole time the focus of the rest of the group should be on the person doing the addressing and not the person receiving. At the end of the address, the person receiving says "thank you" in as plain a tone as possible. If there is any emotional intonation, they should take a moment and say it again. This should go around the circle with everyone taking a turn; it should be easy to find something positive to say at the least.

This may feel very new-agey or ridiculous to you and I won't lie in saying that it works one hundred percent of the time, but there are some aspects of the withhold circle that are worth noting. First, it opens up a forum for people to get things off their chest. This includes saying the good things that we don't usually take time to say. Secondly, it has a structure and vocabulary to help create safety for speaking unabashedly. Thirdly, it creates safety for those receiving the comment by putting the group's focus on the one speaking, rather than listening.

Once a forum is created and the air is cleared, there could be an improvement in attitude—sometimes people just need to be heard and know that they are heard so that they can feel valued. The forum might, however, be the first step to help direct you toward the trouble areas that need to be addressed further. In this stage, responsibility needs to be assigned. For example, the issue could be that rehearsals take too long to get started because members enter casually, sometimes with food in hand, while certain people are rushing to get to rehearsal and be ready to go on time. This is healthy to share as it can help dispel certain misconceptions that are undoubtedly in play and help create a new contract. The first misconception is that the performer is alone in feeling this waste of time. Others probably feel the same way but also feel alone in this feeling. The cycle is continuous until the silence is broken. The second common misconception is that the majority of the group likes the status quo and would be angry if it was disturbed. This keeps the more professional improvisers from pushing the others to be less casual. If this went on not being discussed, chances are that this performer would adopt the others' bad habits rather than the other way around (now we have that opportunity). The casual players need to acknowledge that they do dawdle at the top of rehearsal and in acknowledging that take on the challenge in order to change that pattern. Equally, the performers who are ready to go need to take on the challenge of initiating the start of rehearsal. Now that the issue has been discussed, they can engage others in warm-ups or start an improv exercise to get things going.

The final step for dealing with the discontent is creating an out for a performer, which brings us to our final issue.

FIRING PERFORMERS

Not casting an extremely talented person because they are going to be high maintenance to deal with, is THE BEST reason to not cast someone.

—Joe Bill

Firing should be a last resort for any director/performer relationship but it also needs to be an option. Many directors hate the idea of losing a really good performer and are willing to go well out of their way to accommodate them, to a point where it's detrimental to the troupe. I have seen the biggest egos of my generation grow larger by having everything spoon-fed to them as a member of a troupe. This creates a dangerous environment that allows them to take advantage of you as an authority, showboat at the expense of the other players and more.

My advice is to always look at the big picture. A group's success should not hinge upon the participation of one or two individuals. That is not a strong structure from which to build. Improv groups' dynamics are strongest when everyone is equal or focused on lifting each other up. If a good player is allowed certain leniencies, it can rub the other players the wrong way and create a bad precedent of how the group operates that is hard to erase later.

The B-52s reached success after losing Ricky Wilson. The Who did their greatest hits after losing Keith Moon. The Rolling Stones continued without Brian Jones. Metallica grew without Dave Mustaine. The Red Hot Chili Peppers without Hillel Slovak. You get the idea. Recognize that the group is an entity that will survive, despite any casting change.

There are some people who are just never going to get it and that's not your fault.

—Dan O'Connor

****

Hopefully, this chapter has alleviated your stress, if only slightly, about dealing with issues within your group. At the very least, take comfort in the fact that we have all had to deal with these ripples and we have all found ways to survive them.

CHAPTER 11: WORKING WITH A MIXED GROUP

Improv classes I have taught have been a mixed bag of experiences, intentions and personalities. In some classes, I have had students who are doing improv for the very first time, playing side by side with veterans who have been improvising for ten years or more. Sometimes, the newcomers are extremely reserved. Sometimes, the veterans are overbearing with their knowledge, to a point of extreme cynicism. Some classes have students looking to get into film and television, while others were just looking to liven up their 9-to-5 jobs. How does an instructor address all these different needs without being distracted by them? In *Breaking Down the Work*, we talked about how to unify the different philosophies. Now, let us look at how best to bridge the gaps of intention and experience.

EXPERIENCE LEVELS

Most improv schools offer a tiered program of numbered levels. Most need to as a way to track their students, gauge how performance-ready they are and make sure that they are introduced to the artform (particularly their style or approach) in a way that is consistent and accessible.

For now, we are going to look at the only two levels that matter: (1) those who have never improvised before, and (2) everyone else. Just as any scene is about making that initial choice, any improv career starts as soon as that first scene is out of the way. From that moment on, if the improviser is committed, it becomes a continual process of learning that will constantly change direction with each new approach and influence.

As we saw in *Giving Notes and Challenges*, there is a way to challenge students of all experience levels in their scenework. Give an open invitation to try any challenge issued during a workshop. No one's toolbox is above expansion.

THE FIRST SCENE...EVER

The most attractive thing about improvising is the limitless freedom of it. Anything can be created at any moment. This exact freedom, however, is the same thing that can terrify the new improviser. When you have no limit of options, how do you decide on just one?

You can see it on a person's face when they are about to do their first improv scene—the trepidation, a self-consciousness that is usually accompanied by a darting about of the eyes. This is because they are not sure what to focus on. They don't yet understand the idea of just making things up on the spot and following the scene where it goes. The reaction to this plays out different ways in the improvisation from person to person. Many go into a mode of heavy questioning, hoping their scene partner will help them through the experience. Many just stand there and repeat information given to them. The new improviser is desperate for a focus.

When I encounter first-timers in my workshops, I give them a challenge right off the bat, before I have seen them do a single scene. The best one to give is for them to turn to their scene partner at the top of each scene and say "You are _____!" This may feel mechanical to them at first, but it helps. You are giving the new improviser a starting point from which they can create their own ideas. "You are beautiful!" "You are a bum!" "You are so messy!" "You are standing on my dog's tail!" Whatever they say, respond to it with "Great, say it again!" to which they will add emphasis. They have now offered information at the top of the scene, rather than waiting to see what information unfolds that they should run with. Not only that but they are now endowing the other person and doing so through the point of view of a character.

This challenge comes from my philosophy of what makes scenes work, the establishing of a strong dynamic between the two characters. You can create challenges complementary to your own approach on improvisation similar to how we created challenges to change up individual performer's patterns. What challenge can you impose on the top of the new improviser's scene if you want to ensure the strongest character choice? An improviser with an acting background will do better with a Bad Celebrity Impersonation challenge than a non-performer who might do better with adapting their physicality to bring variety.

GROUPING BY INTENTION

Knowing what a student is looking to get out of a workshop goes a long way toward meeting those expectations. I have taught retirees looking to try something new, lawyers looking to gain more confidence, public speakers looking to be more spontaneous and marketing executives looking to be more creative. When they are mixed with the more common acting types, it becomes a fun challenge to adapt for them.

The key place for adaptation is in the notes. There is not much point to giving the lawyer notes on narrative. If their want is to gain confidence, then I am going to focus more on their character choices. Where they choose to back down in a scene or where they choose to commit more aggressively will more evidently affect other areas of their life and work.

There is a concern of slowing down the lesson to the detriment of the more advanced players. As directors, we need to learn what notes should be individualized and what notes can be explored as a group, and to strike a balance between them. Sometimes, when we make a note generally, we can take the pressure off the improviser who would otherwise be singled out. This is helpful in guiding your more self-conscious players, but if done too often or unnecessarily it can sidetrack a group. Some notes need to be given directly, especially when the issue is an obvious one.

The other thing to watch for is that as a leader you are continually progressive, that you do not linger on any one note for too long. Ultimately, improv is about the doing and we want to give the players as much time to play with our ideas as possible. It is also the best way for us to learn as directors what needs to be done next.

When I lead a workshop, I break it up into parts that I push to a point that I want made, milestones that I hit along the course of the session. For instance, perhaps the first milestone is about taking initiative. I have all the improvisers do scenes that last no more than fifteen seconds, putting pressure on them to present an idea for the scene more quickly. My focus is less on having a variety of opening choices at first and more on getting out there quick, helping those improvisers who need it with challenges that will get them to commit sooner in the scene. The next milestone might involve character. Now that we are making stronger initiations, we look at how we can make choices that are specific to a certain character. We are now moving out of the realm of pure instinct and mixing in a little analysis as we start to be aware of previous choices so that we can vary them in the coming scenes. I might direct them to do specific imitations (animals, celebrities, genres) or have them lead with different parts of the body each time to foster variety.

THE DEFAULT

Every improviser has a default setting for their work that comes up when their guard is up. It is whatever is the most comfortable for the performer to do at that time. Many times this default setting means playing very closely to who they are as a person. Often there is a set body language. I worked with one woman who would enter every scene standing center stage, looking at her scene partner, with her arms folded across her chest. This is the choice that she would make at the top of every scene, which would produce the same energy for her characters, usually a defiant one. Another default setting is part of being an adaptive improviser, which we discussed in the sidecoaching chapter—there are many times that I have seen a performer shoot out of the backline into a scene and then make a sudden turn so as to better see what their partner is adding to the scene.

Sometimes, a performer needs to be given permission to slack on certain aspects of the work so that they can train other muscles. It is similar to how in physical therapy a patient needing to rehabilitate a limb is given the opportunity to exercise in a pool, so that the pressure of weight is taken off, and they can increase their mobility. Giving the improviser permission to never look at their partner in a string of scenes will open them up to other places where they can throw their focus. (Note: if you use this in a workshop, it's best to give the fixed gaze challenge from the notes chapter so that the performer will be more focused on what they *are* looking at rather than what they are not looking at.) It feels weird for them to go against what they feel they are "supposed to do" in a scene and I am sure it similarly feels weird for you to direct them to do so, but there are times when aiming for perfection becomes too much of a distraction.

Players may only have defaults in certain areas of their work. Try this with one of your best players. Ask him to do a character with a Japanese accent performing a simple task, such as placing an order at a fast food restaurant. Now ask him to do a different Japanese character, and then a third, and a fourth. Most improvisers will do the gruff-voiced Japanese male character that they learned from genre games where the suggestion is Kabuki. Most of them have never had extended contact with Japanese culture or seen a

Kabuki play—only the watered-down improvised versions that have been passed down as a shorthand. This is an example of the go-tos that we all have in our vocabulary that we could stand to work away from.

PLAYING UGLY

After physical warm-ups, I usually run a quick breathing exercise to help people let go of any baggage from earlier in their day before jumping into the improv. Everyone closes their eyes, takes in a deep breath, holds it for three seconds, and exhales with a sound. We repeat, this time letting out the breath with a sound from "the bowels of Hell." We repeat one final time, now releasing the breath with a note. More often than not there is a significant pause before the note comes.

This simple breathing exercise serves as a metaphor. There is no hesitation when making Hellish sounds because in asking for it that way, I have allowed them to be ugly. But a musical note, even though it wasn't presented as such, has a connotation of needing to be perfect. The improvisers are suddenly self-conscious of their sound choice and let others start first so that they can jump in through harmonization.

The same thing happens with beginning improvisers. They usually approach the scenework gingerly, trying to achieve an ideal they have in their minds. However, this results in less energetic choices, which keeps them from that ideal. Rehearsals and workshops should be a time to experiment with ideas. Players need to be allowed to play ugly in a classroom setting so that they can get to their choices more quickly and more viscerally. When they have gotten that out, then they can learn how to refine the choices they've made, rather than edit themselves beforehand.

The best way to help them there is to give them permission to do badly. When someone is allowed to fail, they make the choices bigger since there is no pressure and, thus, no holding back. Sometimes you can give the player specific things to focus on that takes a specific pressure off of them, the way we did in countering the default. An improviser who is thinking very carefully about what they are saying and hesitating in their dialogue can be given permission to talk in gibberish in all their scenes or permission to say the same things over and over again. This will divert their attention from what they think the scene needs, to other areas that will more strongly fuel their choices.

[There are] teachers who are like, "What if you have that one student and they're just horrible and they're just not going to get it? How do you tell a student that it's time to hang it up quick and forget about it?" And I know teachers who raise this question all the time at teacher's meetings. "I feel like we're ripping this person off, taking their money and they just don't get it, they're never going to get it, blah blah blah."...I don't believe as a teacher you're in the position to make that decision for someone. This goes back to when I was a kid, something that happened between me and a coach, where it's like dreams die hard and it's not up to me to decide when your dream is over. You will come to that realization in good time and it will be either hugely rewarded or it will be a very painful moment in your life but that moment that comes in that person's life, when that moment comes, it's up to them. It's not up to me, and my role is to help them as much as I can in that moment when our paths cross and what happens after that is up to them, it's not up to me.

—*Mark Sutton*

CHAPTER 12: WORKING WITH CHILDREN

> I first taught 4th – 6th graders, I believe, when I was about 17 years old. I found I had strong ideas and I loved doing it, though I also remember having a headache after every class because it demanded such focus and investment, and teaching was scary, though exciting.
>
> —*Shira Piven*

Working within a classroom, you might have a group that has signed up for your class—an optimal condition—or perhaps you are being forced upon them. They may be familiar with the performing arts through personal experience or by watching *Whose Line Is it Anyway?* or they may have had no exposure whatsoever. Perhaps they are enthusiastic or perhaps they are scared. Regardless of the circumstances, there are certain givens.

The biggest thing going for you is the guaranteed fact that you are an alternative to what these children normally do during the day and what they are used to. Most classrooms that I have seen while working as a visiting artist in the New York City public school system are overcrowded and overloaded with requirements, mandatory testing and uninspired art projects. The supplies and environments are usually sub-par. The staff varies in experience and enthusiasm. You are a break in the routine for these children, and that helps a lot in winning them over in your first meeting. The other kids divide into two groups: those who are too shy to participate and those who are not shy but can't direct their enthusiasm into the improvisation.

PROVIDING FOR A CREATIVE ENVIRONMENT

Elementary level children are naturally expressive, mostly in a selfish sense. They love most to create something and feel that it is unique and they alone could have created it. What others think is secondary to their own joy. As they grow older, fewer of them retain this creative enthusiasm. This playfulness becomes dulled by obligations, the pressures of adolescence, and the structures of authority that oversee them. They become confused on how to be an individual and to still be accepted.

Many improv teachers go into the classroom with the idea of first covering the "rules" of improvisation: the idea of yes-anding, not denying and making your partner look good. These are important tenets of improv but they are huge, overwhelming concepts that can work against younger children's creative tendencies and can turn off the older ones. The way in is through their own selfish desires. Give the children room to play how they choose to play, to show off if they want to, and then refine it as you go along.

When you are working with the teacher, this can cause some friction, because some teachers need to keep absolute control over the classroom and spontaneity doesn't gel with that goal. These teachers may already be resentful of your presence as it takes away from their class time which they could devote to fulfilling requirements or having the children catch up on lessons.

When I work with children, I try to be most mindful that (a) they open up to the new experiences I am offering, and (b) the experience doesn't dredge up a lot of negative-based work. The first thing I always do is introduce two rules:

1. Everything is 100% correct.
2. Everything must be 100% original.

In regard to the first rule, let me stress that I mean all choices are 100% correct. The children need to feel ongoing support, or they will turn off to what you have to show. They also need to have fun and that gets stifled easily when you place restrictions upon them. Of course, this means allowing for the chance of inappropriate content. Certain types of content creep into the scenework that are usually considered taboo: drug deals, violent acts, sex, etc. The normal impulse is to show these choices as wrong and steer the kids towards more PC topics. This does not, however, contribute to a creative environment.

You must always praise the children, keep them impassioned about their choices and then challenge them to make the widest range of choices possible. At first, their range will be limited, pulling from what they see on television and in movies, or what they think is "cool" to bring up in front of the other kids.

One way to deal with these instances is to enforce the idea that everything must be 100% original. The primary reason for this second rule is to keep the kids from simply playing out moments from well-known movies or TV shows in place of creating their own ideas, but it can also be useful in minimizing the inappropriate. For instance, if two children do a scene that involves a subject like a fistfight, praise them on the scene without any ifs, ands, or buts. Then call two more students up for a scene with the preface of "Let's see another great scene but remember, we want everything to be 100% original so let's have this scene be about anything but fighting." (You will notice that I avoided using words like "no" or "not" which could put a child on the defensive.) If there were other prominent elements in the scene—like if the fight was over a dog—then you can list those more innocuous objects with the taboo ones, adding to it as you go through more scenes. "Okay, let's see another great scene but this time about anything but fighting, dogs, spaceships..." Now the children are in an environment that is creatively more free. The children who try to get a reaction by bringing up such content, get praised instead. Those children who are limited or self-conscious who bring up these topics because they are easy or cool, will similarly come out on top and be more able to push farther each time.

Another way is to separate the emotional choice from the content. For example, I have witnessed many scenes about drug deals. When it happens, I congratulate the kids on what they did well. Sometimes, I will confide in them that I wouldn't want the principal to walk in on a scene like that, and they'll often respect that. Mostly, I have them repeat the scene a few times, replacing the drugs with some innocuous object while still regarding it as if it were drugs. Now, we have a series of scenes where one character has an extreme and desperate need for puppies or pound cake or socks. The kid will enjoy the absurdity of the results and will most likely be brimming over with ideas for substitute drugs.

Similarly, when dealing with a violent interaction, commend them on their emotional commitment, then create a challenge. For instance, if the scene involved one character shooting the other, have the kids take turns initiating harmless actions while their scene partners still react as if they were being shot.

Some topics are tougher to sweep past because they could be hurtful to another child in the classroom. The focus needs to be on empowering the target rather than giving extra attention to the provocateur.

My proudest improv moment is when I was doing an artist residency with a group of first-graders in an NYC elementary school. The focus of the workshop was to introduce the kids to improvisation to help them in dealing with conflicts. As part of the class we did an exercise created by my friend Steve Wacker called Superheroes. One child would get up in front of the class and would be given the name of a made-up superhero. The children would then embody that character, tell us about their powers or origin. One child who got up was given the name Big Ears by a classmate which, I could tell, was a personal jab at the kid. The whole class laughed but my volunteer ran with it. He created a great character that could fly using his ears, and who by flapping them could make huge gusts of wind that would knock over his opponents. The class erupted in laughter again, but this time they were laughing with him instead of at him.

Other topics that have come up are those of misogyny and otherness, particularly in addressing homosexuality as a joke, usually from older kids. The impulse is to explain the reasons why such choices are wrong or hurtful but in doing so you may lose some of the ground that you have gained by being outside the authority system they deal with regularly. Any serious discussions are better served when preceded by a substitution, as we did before when dealing with content of drug use or violence. For instance, a derogatory term can be replaced with some made up term that is used as a derogatory term. Or, the children can play with delivering what are normally pleasant terms as if they were derogatory (i.e., saying "sweetheart" in a venomous tone). By treating it like any other choice that could be made, we are giving the child who used the offensive term a chance to devalue the choice for himself, not for moral reasons but for the selfish reason of wanting to be the most original and imaginative person in the room. Once it is devalued, it is easier to address the moral side of the issue. Also, by doing this we are separating the word, often powerfully charged with controversy, from the intention of the person saying it. If you still feel the need to address the psychology of racism and misogyny, this will provide a good starting point for the discussion.

THE ARC OF THE LESSON

Many teachers look to have the lessons lead up to a performance. Realize that this creates more difficulties without always being worth it. As I mentioned earlier, there are a huge number of factors that go into classroom management on the high school level or younger. A performance in front of their peers can add unnecessary pressure to the kids who are still unsure of their improv skills and for you, as you're trying to help them find their way. You are already dealing with egos, emotional problems and petty conflicts. Granted, these are present in adult groups as well, but at least it's balanced with performance experience and an understanding of what a successful show requires.

What is the purpose of your course and how does a live performance fit? If your purpose is to simply introduce new skills to the kids, then a performance isn't mandatory. If you are required by the supervisors or administrators of the program to have an end result, there are other ways they can be accomplished:

1. Bring in a video camera and improvise short films with the kids. This will give you tighter control over the performance. The children will not have to deal with the anxiety of performing live and they will have a keepsake of the class. School administrators often appreciate this because it is a tangible product that they can show off when they are reviewed. (NOTE: You often need to get parental consent before videotaping children.)

2. Produce writing (short plays, skits, etc.) based on the improvisation. This tends to make many children less self-conscious.

3. Do a scaled-down performance of a few games in the classroom in front of the administrators and/or parents. It is completely possible to pull off a live performance but it is not often necessary. Ultimately, you want to make sure that it is because the children would benefit from it and not to serve any other agenda. I have prepared many high school students proudly for performance, but not without giving myself the chance to properly assess their potential and foster it to a higher level.

The point is to find what the kids most need and do the project that enables that. Kids who are learning to work as a team or to be creative or to deal with conflicts can do so more easily without an audience. If there are other parties that need to be satisfied—the principal, the teachers or the parents—then modify the environment to provide for them, but make sure they have their eye on what is best for the kids as well.

CLASS ORGANIZATION

I cannot predict how any child is going to respond to me or the activities I run. Truthfully, there are too many factors that go into a classroom setup, from the specifics of the environment I previously mentioned to the aspects of each individual child's home life. There are, however, ways to safeguard in your favor starting with those who are visiting artists at public or private schools.

1. Structure with adaptability. Kids will change focus on a whim and you need to be ready to change with them. You need to have a tightly planned agenda for each class and, in addition, a stockpile of games that you can whip out at a moment's notice. Group games with simple structures allow for the most opportunity for personal expression.

2. Keep things moving. The key thing to watch in a classroom is the energy levels, when they go up and when they go down. Have kids fill out as many roles as possible (i.e., lights, coloring, notes, making sketches). Also, by doing shorter games you can allow for greater turnover in all the roles. The kids will also be more involved because there will be calls for their wonderful suggestions more often. Kids want to be a part of whatever is fun. That sense of enthusiasm is how you know how well you are doing your job.

3. Avoid the vocabulary they are desensitized to. Kids will get hyper and the words freeze, halt, and stop have lost their power because they have been used so much. Early on, stand them up as a group and teach them, each in their own spot to "pose for a picture." They will now take all the energy they have and focus it into posing as still as possible. The more ridiculous the pose, the better, because that means they are putting more energy into it. Now, if at any time during the class they start getting rambunctious, call out for everyone to "pose for a picture" and they will respond

to it because it was introduced in a positive context. For every order that you need there is a more successful counterpart that will challenge them to do something that will fulfill their needs without stifling them.

4. <u>Ally yourself strongly with the teacher</u>. The teacher knows the particulars of each child's background as it tends to affect the classroom dynamic. The teacher should also play the role of disciplinarian so you don't have to. Teachers can vary from feeling enthusiastically optimistic about your program to being downright resentful of the time being taken away from getting "real" work done.

PLAYING GAMES AND LETTING THE RULES GO

Kids are getting to be very fast-paced. The television shows they watch and the games they play contribute to an already present desire for constant stimulus, especially in the stifling confines of school. You need to be mindful of their energy levels and learn to adapt with their sudden changes.

In preparing to work with children, it is most important to have an overly structured agenda that you can stray from. On the one hand, you don't want to run out of what to do and have to flounder for some filler games. On the other hand, you don't want to commit to a string of lessons that the children are clearly not reacting to. The beginning of the workshops are the key to their success. Engage them directly and immediately and they will follow you anywhere. This is not done by creating a foundation of rules but by jumping directly into something fun that they can get involved in. One game that I have used for this purpose is Big Bag, where I would mime dragging a big bag to the center front of the room. Then I would rummage around in the big bag and pull out an imaginary object that I would start playing with. All of this works best without dialogue, using sounds instead (such as grunts while dragging the bag or whistling while finding an object). Then I try to get the kids to guess what the object is while I use it. After a few times of doing this on my own, I pull up kids to reach into the big bag. The simplest games are the ones like this where it is so simple that you do not even need to explain the rules. Play the game and let them join in.

When I visit public schools to work with the children in their classrooms, I often have them play Blind Alphabet. In groups of six, they would try to go consecutively from A to Z, each person saying only one letter at a time, though in no particular speaking order, with their eyes closed. If more than one child says a letter at the same time, the group has to start again from A. I would go from group to group to challenge them on how far through the alphabet they could get. If I let them, the children would play this game for my entire visit. Blind Alphabet was a phenomenon that they could not get enough of because they would respond strongly to easy structures that they can excel at. The kids like Blind Alphabet because it has only a couple of simple rules and allows for do-overs. The teachers appreciate it because the focus is on developing their listening and cooperative skills. I like the game for how it uses large groups of the kids at once (for multiple visits, expand the size of the groups each time to test their skills on a higher level.)

Kids enjoy the idea of routines and rituals, even if they don't always appreciate the work involved or the lesson behind them. They respond to whatever excitement you put behind the exercise, so it needs to be high. They do even better when you give them room to create within the routine, once again allowing them to be selfish. Another game I have played with kids is Information Booth.

Get a suggestion of an item one would buy at the mall, such as shoes or candy. Line the kids up and have them approach you one at a time, in character, to ask you where that item can be found. Once you direct them, they exit. The focus is on how to creatively do that same simple task in a number of different ways (different walks, different voices, different phrasing).

Along the way, words can be fed to the kids to inspire new characters. Start with concrete ideas that can easily be applied to character work, such as occupations or emotions. From there you can challenge them further with animal suggestions for physicality or musical instruments to mimic different vocals which will require them to adapt the idea to fit. Finally, you can toss out more indirect terms such as cloud, water or barbed wire.

THE POWER STRUGGLE

If I am going to expect my students to participate, particularly in workshop situations where they are being forced to participate, I need to create an environment where they will not feel self-conscious. Classrooms can be an overcrowded, claustrophobic experience that puts kids in a more survival-based mindset. They learn from each other the quick and easy ways to get attention or demonstrate power over others. This can sometimes involve humiliating or physically attacking others.

They are constantly on their guard against each other or against the authority figures who, in their own quick and easy ways of demonstrating power, too often point out faults or stifle actions. This is why the rule "Everything is 100% correct" is so important to maintain but incredibly difficult to adhere to.

Here is something that has worked as an example of manipulating the energy of the room when it is working against you. I was in a classroom of third graders where I was having trouble getting the students' attention to start the session. There were a number of side conversations going on and very few kids had their focus on me. The instinct would be to raise one's voice to get the focus back, but that does not always work. In fact, it can further feed their lack of attention as you have now labelled yourself as an authoritarian in the mode that they are all too familiar with. Instead, make what you are doing intriguing enough to earn their attention. In this case, I started whispering, "The King! The King!" to the few kids who were already focused on me, encouraging them to whisper it in return. As this continued, more kids were enlisted into this activity, some by me, some by the children who were already involved. The activity now developed a club-like aura of which the kids wanted to be a part. If any of the kids started shouting the word "The King" I would run to them and whisper it directly to them in the character of someone who was scared of the The King rather than making it as if I just wanted them to keep their voices down. Soon I had the class working with me, their focus was on me as they were doing something that they wanted to be a part of without knowing why and looking to me to see what would happen next. And since they were all whispering, the volume was low enough to give further instructions if I needed to. Instead, I started to physically transform myself into a royal figure to take them to the next level of the game. Then I approached one of the kids, removed my crown, quickly switching out of my regal posturing, and placed the crown on his head, signifying it was his turn to be king. I would quickly run to take his seat as he got up to further enforce the idea of taking turns. If he didn't get what was going on, I could easily begin murmuring "The King!"—this time with him as the focus.

In this short amount of time, I have now earned the kids' trust, gotten them focused and warmed up and taught them how to improvise a single, simple idea. The key is to be creative in how you engage the children while doing specific activities and looking like you are having fun performing that activity. It is comparable to the story of how Tom Sawyer tricked the children in the neighborhood to paint the fence for him while convincing them that it was fun to do so.

APPENDIX A: EXERCISES

Don't rely on book exercises too much. Sure, the first exercises you do, you should take from books. [But] books are never going to fully translate what an exercise is like. Instead, you should make exercises up as much as possible. The specific problems people are having, try to make an exercise up to tackle it. You'll have more success and you'll become a better coach the more you can create your exercises.

—Kevin Mullaney

Whenever I teach my directing intensives, I put it to the students to lead the warm-ups. As a result, I have been part of more rounds of Zip Zap Zop than I care to remember. Mind you, it is a fun little warm-up and when people remember that there is a specific reason for playing it, they can get a lot from the exercise.

Meanwhile, here are a number of exercises that have served me well and which help cover a number of bases. Some of them, I created through the years, though undoubtedly there are parallel versions that were created elsewhere in the world. Other exercises were learned through other improvisers, some of which were passed on to them. Rather than try to track down the origins of exercises — a near impossible task — I credit the improviser from whom I learned it, where applicable.

Exercises marked with asterisks (**) signify that they are especially good games to play with children of a young age.

AMALGAM
Focus: Group awareness

Instructions: Get in a circle. Make eye contact with each other. Don't focus on anyone for too long. Try to take in the entire group. Take in everyone's physicality all at once while maintaining eye contact. Incorporate what you find into your own physicality. Exaggerate these characteristics. Continue to incorporate the new things that develop and exaggerate them.

Variation: For larger groups, separate into two or more circles of at least five people each. As they do the Amalgam exercise, have them make their circles larger and larger until they eventually overlap. The focus is now on each player keeping an awareness of only their group.

CHARACTER KARAOKE (A Hot Spot Variation)
Focus: Character

Hot Spot is an exercise from *Truth in Comedy* where the players get in a circle, with one person stepping into the center to sing a song. The players in the circle jump in to sing a related song, pushing that person out of the center. In this variation, the first song is sung in character. The type of person who would sing "Fight For Your Right (to Party)" is different from the one who would sing "I Get a Kick Out of You." The players on the outside jump in to the center, but this time do a monologue using the same character from the song but without referencing the song at all. Another player jumps in with a new song inspired by the monologue and so forth—song in character, same character doing monologue, song with new character, same character doing new monologue, etc.

The use of songs is a great way to inject an instant philosophy into your character creations. The ear cutting scene from *Reservoir Dogs* says a lot about Michael Madsen's character, even more so because he is singing "Stuck in the Middle With You" while doing it.

Things to watch for: Dancing to a song is different from character movement and tends to be more unfocused. Dancing can also be a sign that the player is not making specific character choices but is moving for the sake of adding movement. Sidecoach them to focus on an aspect of the dancing as we did in the Extend/Continue exercise (i.e., flailing arms, side-to-side movement, etc.), and the gesturing will gel into more of a character choice.

As the exercise continues, the players may abandon the idea of singing in favor of having their characters speak the lyrics instead and need to be nudged back. Maintaining the use of melodies helps increase the variety of characters by introducing new rhythms of speech. When the vocalization of the songs get carried over into the monologues, certain words or syllables are held, adding surprising character information.

COMPLEMENTARY SCULPTURES

Focus: Physicality

This game has been attributed to Keith Johnstone. One person takes an abstract pose in the center. A second person makes a complementary pose. First person says "Thank you" and leaves. Third person enters and second person says "Thank you" and leaves, and so forth.

Things to watch for: Make sure players keep their faces and feet engaged for the most dynamic possible poses. See that the sculptures occasionally play with distance rather than constantly being tight compositions.

I'M SO...

Focus: Action/Reaction

Form a circle. One person turns to the next and vocalizes a direct action to them (e.g. "I give you a birthday gift"). That person vocalizes an emotional reaction starting with "I'm so..." (e.g., "I'm so pleased.") They then turn to the next person and vocalize a direct action based on their emotion, but unrelated to the previous action (e.g., "I help you move into your new apartment"). If they have trouble coming up with an action, direct them to repeat their emotional response, heightening it each time. For example:

1st Person:	I give you the finger.
2nd Person:	(to 3rd person) I am so shocked. I am so shocked. I am so shocked that I don't see you and bump into you, knocking you down.
3rd Person:	(to 4th person) I am so pissed that I forget that it's our anniversary...
4th Person:	(to 5th person) I am so sad that I cry on your shoulder...

Things to watch for: Players will sometimes confuse states of being (such as confusion) with emotions. These can lead to emotions (the Incredible Hulk's confusion leads to anger while Scooby Doo's confusion leads to fear).

IMPROVISED BOARD GAME**

Focus: Scene building

Get the group in a circle (four to five people per circle is optimal, though it can be done with any number). Have them lay their hands on an imaginary table so that they can all agree on its height. One player then begins playing a made-up board game without using words or sound effects (other sounds are fine). Each player takes their turn at the game creating details as they go along. How is the progress of the game measured (by winning cards, movement across the board, etc.)? If there is movement, is it one path (like Monopoly) or multiple paths (Trivial Pursuit)? One game piece, or many (Chinese Checkers)? Dice? Spinner? Pop-o-matic bubble? After a couple of rounds, ask everyone to simultaneously point at the person who is winning the board game and then the person who is in last place.

This game is very obvious in its metaphor of scenework: there is a game being played, with rules that are created on the spot, that everyone agrees on and adds to, people play different roles (winner, loser), and it comes to a logical end.

Things to watch for: The key thing is seeing how the players decide the winner without speaking. There will be those who are overly polite, letting others win by not asserting how they are doing.

MACHINE CHALLENGE**
Focus: Teamwork

Break the children up into groups of five to six. The groups will each be challenged to construct a machine using their bodies as the parts without communicating verbally. You will give the groups a specific machine to create, like a helicopter or blender or stapler, something with as many parts as possible. If there are three groups or more, allow the kids to take turns on different machines. If there are four or more groups, it might be better to make the challenge a time race and see which group can create the one machine most quickly.

Things to watch for: There will be some kids, with an enthusiasm for "winning," who will drag other kids into the machine and physically pose them. You want to encourage the enthusiasm and have the child reroute that energy into making a very clear choice for herself that the other kids can build around.

PASS THE PHRASE
Focus: Heightening

The members of The Corduroy Rogers taught me this exercise (crediting Jill Bernard for showing it to them) where one person walks up to another in the circle and says a mundane line of dialogue. That person then approaches a third, the third approaches a fourth, and so on, and so on, each using the same line. With each repetition, the delivery of the previous actor (including the walk) gets exaggerated.

POISON-ARM SAMURAI
Focus: Teamwork

This was a physical game that I learned from Michael Rock while working with him in NY Theatresports.

Form a circle. Instruct the group that they have poison blades on each arm going from the pinky to the elbow. When someone is touched by this blade, they instantaneously die. They can, however, block a blade with their own blade. To ensure safety and to make the battle that will ensue the most dynamic, the exercise is done in slow motion. One person should lead the pace at first by going through a couple of samurai poses in slow motion and having everyone mirror them. The leader then shouts "Battle begin!" which is the cue for everyone to go for the kill.

Things to watch for: The natural impulse is to try to win the fight and be the last one standing. In truth, the object is to have the most gorgeous death possible. Giving the players this focus will result in a lot more fun swordplay with near-misses and tricky blocks and overly emotional deaths. If people are having trouble letting the idea of winning go, give them a number order according to which they will die.

PROCEDURE GAME**
Focus: Building narrative

Form a circle. One person speaks and acts out the first step on a list of improvised instructions (e.g., dig a hole, open the box, etc.). Everyone then repeats and acts out the instruction. People take turns adding another instruction to the list. After each new instruction the entire list gets repeated and acted out.

This game is helpful for storytelling with kids who tend to add extraneous story elements rather than building off what came before.

REGARD/RESPOND/REACT
Focus: Action/Reaction

People break up into pairs. One physicalizes a direct action like offering a hand for a handshake or entering the other person's space. Their partner then goes through the three stages of the exercise's title:

1. REGARD—his is taking in the other person's offer and focusing on key elements. For instance, if offered a handshake, I might stare at the hand or the "audience" with uncertainty. (Note: Uncertainty is not an emotional response but a state of being that leads to one.)

2. RESPONSE—Now an emotional reaction is made, such as being fearful of the outstretched hand.

3. REACTION—Now an action is taken based on the emotion, such as stepping away from the other person in fear.

This exercise should be done wordlessly, to best see the differences between the three stages.

Variations: Have the players stay on one of the stages much longer than the others. What does it feel like to over-emote in response to every little thing? How far can a physical reaction be taken? Similarly, it is fun and challenging to eliminate stages. The classic Commedia fool only reacts without a need to regard or emotionally respond first.

*SUPERHEROES I***
Focus: Energy

This is an energy pass warm-up where each player in the circle, in their turn, says a word or phrase with a movement. It should be something that can be easily repeated. After everyone has created a movement, go around the circle two more times to repeat the creations. To begin the passing, one person does their phrase and movement and then someone else's. The second person does their own and then the movement of someone else in the circle.

Things to watch for: There will be the occasional hesitation when someone has forgotten one of the other players' phrase and movement. The focus, however, is not on memory but on energy. Coach the players that it is perfectly alright if they do the same pass over and over again. As the warm-up progresses, the repetition will make things easier.

Variations: The warm-up can also be used as a means to learn names by substituting them for the phrase. It is particularly good for a first class or a rehearsal where new members are being introduced.

SUPERHEROES II**
Focus: Empowerment

A player gives the person to their left a made-up superhero name whose powers they must define in the hero's persona.

Things to watch for: This exercise feels daunting at first but once it gets going, the momentum builds on its own. Get the players to step out right away and repeat the superhero name they have been given as soon as it's given. Have them repeat the name when stepping back as well to help people who fade themselves out when they are not happy about their choices.

This game has worked exceptionally well with children in performance workshops as well as in conflict resolution.

WORD-AT-A-TIME PROVERBS
Focus: Creating a positive energy

Form a circle. Create a fortune cookie proverb with each person contributing one word as you go around the circle. The most important part of the exercise is that when a proverb is finished, everyone must simultaneously let out a big, awe-inspired "AAH!" This is a great game to play with kids to illustrate the idea of Yes And.

Things to watch for: Some people have a tendency to add filler words such as "will" or "might" rather than add a good descriptive verb; or phrases like "decided to" will precede an action rather than just jumping to the action. When this comes up, I challenge the players to go short and pithy and they will jump in with stronger choices that will add more information.

APPENDIX B: STORIES FROM THE FRONT LINES

In the course of writing this book, I spoke to dozens of talented improv directors and teachers with a wide range of experiences. Rather than shoehorn pieces of those interviews into the preceding chapters, the unused portions have been collected here under different topics. My hope is that by reviewing these anecdotes and thoughts you will fully see the common ground that all of us have trod and will continue to go tread.

AWKWARD MOMENTS

Once I was coaching a team in a Meisner-type exercise, making them say, "I love you" to each other. I wasn't paying even attention to the order as the people went through the line, and so I accidentally made my ex-boyfriend and his new girlfriend say "I love you" to each other right in front of me. I felt myself split: it kicked me hard in my jilted heart, but the director part of my brain was pleased with their naturalism. I know the lesson should be don't date other improvisers, but really who else is interesting enough to date?

—Jill Bernard

I was teaching a class two years ago...and I noticed in one of the shows the performers were playing these overly gay characters that were just so over-the-top gay. It was ridiculous. The audience wasn't laughing because it was kind of offensive. So the next day in the class [I was teaching], the same guy was doing the same character and I stopped him and I said "You are doing these characters and you're being so over the top with them. You shouldn't be doing that. And I know you're doing that so that you can make fun of gay people in your character so that no one thinks you're gay. And the thing is, the audience doesn't think you're gay because you're playing gay characters so pull back from it. Play them normal and the audience will appreciate that more. We here in the class, because you're doing those characters, know you're actually gay. The audience will be beyond that so don't worry about it. We know you're gay but the audience doesn't." Everyone laughed, thought it was hilarious. Then I said "You're gay, right?" and he nodded his head and said "Yes, I am gay. My team doesn't know but now that they are in the class, they now know that I am a homosexual. This past weekend I was finally able to tell my parents.

And I am starting to move on and I wasn't expecting to come out on this trip. I am a homosexual." And that is how I outed someone in my class. I actually outed them in front of eighteen other people and it has made its way through all the [Festivals]. Every year someone asks me about it. So this kid can't ever come back to this festival. It's okay to be gay but being outed by his teacher was very shocking to him. And embarrassing for me because I was too much of a smart-ass and made a joke.

—Jeff Griggs

LEARNING FROM THE GREATS

So, this guy walks in, black tapered pants, black work boots, a black leotard turtleneck shirt, horn-rimmed glasses held together by band-aids and safety pins, a ponytail, smoking a cigarette. He walks onto the stage. "I'm Del Close. I just want you all to know that I am going to take over this workshop now. I'm the director and I'm running your workshop. There are a few things that I want to get straight with everyone here. First thing is, I make the rules and you will follow the rules. However, if anybody breaks a rule and it works, I will applaud you. If you break the rule and it doesn't work, I will castigate you. Are we clear? And, by the way, if any of you here think that you can run this workshop better than me, you're welcome to try. Just come up here and say you want to run it and I'll give you a shot. If you're not better than me, I'm coming back up." So, we pretty much knew who Del was at that point.

—Gary Austin, on meeting Del for the first time
when he guest-taught at The Committee.

One time I was sitting having a drink with Martin [de Maat] after a show and someone came up and we got into a conversation about the show and I was bemoaning the fact that the show wasn't exactly right and I didn't feel good about it and Martin just started brushing me with his hand and I thought I had something on me and I said, "Do I have something on me?"and he said, "Yes, you have negativity on you, get it off you, get it off you right now because it doesn't matter." And I was like; "Ah, interesting" and I remember that now. I don't dwell on shows anymore.

—Mark Sutton

I was very fortunate to be in Chicago when I was, there was such a pool of great teachers there to learn from. Marty, Del, Mick. Shira obviously and also an acting teacher here named Lesly Kahn (non-improv but a straight shooter). I remember once Del asked me "What kind of lame ass choice was that?" In the same week he complimented me on how smart my stuff was getting. He was very frank. Shira teaches like she's rifling through her bag looking for her keys. It's amazing because she always finds them. Marty is all about taking care of your partner, Mick complements that by saying the best way to take care of your partner is to take care of yourself first. From Del and Shira I got experimentation. Marty, work with a gentle hand. Mick, great nuts and bolts. Lesly and Del tell it like it is. All of their words continue to fly out of my mouth.

—Todd Stashwick

FIRST TIME TEACHING

My first teaching experience was at a place called Cross Currents Cabaret. That's also where ImprovOlympic started. I was doing the Harold and I was really wanting to start to teach. One day I decided to type out a little sign-up sheet and pass it around to other people in the Improv community at that time. I think it was around 1987. I got about eight people to sign up for a Sunday class. The charge was three dollars a person.

—Mick Napier

I was just so terrified. I did not feel like I had the right to teach anybody how to improvise. Even though I knew how to play the game, I didn't know how to express it. So I went in, pretty much pretending to be Mick. I wore my rattiest jeans. I smoked. I cursed. And I was just trying to channel his brilliance about what to say. But I didn't know how to do it other than to pretend that I was him. So I did. I pretended I was him. People probably looked at me really strangely...The whole thing was terrifying. I got through it and I know that they enjoyed it. So, I feel like, well, I did that one thing.

—Rebecca Sohn

I [was] going to starve to death and the only thing I can think of that I could possibly do is teach a workshop. I had never taught in my life. I had never wanted to teach. I had never thought of being a teacher. But I'm desperate...So, I am faced with twenty-one people, many of them are working actors...I got up in front of the group and I said, "Look, I have never taught. I have no idea if I should teach or not but I'm going to teach for four hours tonight. Nobody owes me any money. It's all free. If you continue the workshop—I'll be here next Monday—come back and you'll start paying me $25 a month starting next week. Tonight's a freebie." Nineteen out of the twenty-one came back. So, I figured, that's pretty good. I can teach.

—*Gary Austin, on his first move to Los Angeles and starting his own class.*

TRYING TO GETTING THROUGH

I was trying to direct these junior high kids last month and I couldn't even direct them to stand in a circle. Seriously, we couldn't form a circle. I realized right away that every improv game and exercise I know would be way too queerball for this group. The most genuinely successful part of the session was when we told a bunch of Your Mama jokes. We played half a game of "Dr. Know It All" where one of the questions was, "Why is everybody gay?" to which I said, "Now, now, only ten percent." Later a fight broke out, and probably I shouldn't have found that as hilarious as I did. "This is B.S." one tiny boy told me. Ah, from the mouths of babes.

—*Jill Bernard*

I had a class in December at Second City that was probably one of the more difficult classes that I have ever had to teach. A ten-person class and I had one guy who was constantly breaking the fourth wall to comment on himself and his own performance. An older guy, probably late forties early fifties who was very self conscious about his own performance. So I had that going on. Then I had a guy who would also break character in the middle of the scene whenever he felt like he was doing something wrong. He'd start laughing and basically want to give up on the scene. Then I had a Korean woman who barely spoke English and when she did it was with a very heavy Korean accent, and she too would look at me and start laughing and ask me straight out in the middle of the scene what she's supposed to do next. Then had an older guy, probably in his sixties, who was very smart and very funny, had great funny ideas and he had a severe, really severe, stuttering problem. So that was basically half of the class and there were times when I taught this class on Monday nights and I would be working during the day on Monday and I would just be like "God I don't want to go down to Second City and teach this class. I would give anything if somebody called me and said this class was cancelled. I do not want to go teach this class." And then I remembered one time Martin said that anytime you have a class, before you walk into the room three times say to yourself I love this class. And I found myself being like "I love this class, I love this class, I love this class," and then you walk in and it's really forced and it's really manipulating your own mindset, but it helps.

—*Mark Sutton*

The worst time I ever had to do a corporate thing, we did it for a group down in I believe it was Alabama, and it was a group of rock quarry workers. These guys had hands and knuckles bigger than my head. These are true hardworking guys out in the field and we're splitting into groups and saying, "Okay, what we're going to do is catch each other when we fall backwards. It's a trust exercise" and they're all looking at us like we're idiots. Well, the structure of this corporate workshop is that each teacher had a group and that we would teach a game, a performance game, and at the end of the session, everyone would perform their game. And we all had a different run-in for this, and I said, all right this is what we're going to do, I'm going to teach you this game and you're going to perform it in front of everybody. And they're like, "What? I don't think so" and they had a lot of reluctance. A friend of mine Don Bardwell...he was in this workshop and he's 6'4" or whatever he is, and a little bit more intimidating, so where for me the guys could just walk over me and be like "shut up," they went up against Don. They didn't literally get in his face, but when he said, "We're going to get together, and we're teach you a game and then you're going to perform it," and two of the guys said, "No we ain't," and he's like, "Ah, all right." They grunted a lot. But the one who had the most success was our friend Deb Downing, who, sweet gal from Texas and she basically turned it around on them and first taught them the game and then they liked it, and they're like, "Hey, this is kind of fun." And she's like, "Great, would you guys—you don't have to, but if you did—would you want to perform it in front of the group?" and they were like, "Yeah, yeah, we'll do that, sure." And that was a great thing about how to handle the group; you can't approach every class the same if you want to get something accomplished.

—*Bob Dassie*

We had this guy who just was the most driving freak from hell and really just unaware of how not good he was, and I used him as an example the first time I ever taught a Directing Class. I let him be in charge. I let him hang himself, so he could see what that felt like. Hopefully he'd learn from it. This particular guy did not learn from it, and what I had to do was replace him in the cast because he just didn't see. He thought everybody else was bad.

—*Dan O'Connor*

PERSONALITIES & NEUROSES

I get phone calls every night, every damn night. I have gone through more breakups than any coach in the world and I have not dated enough people to have to go through this many breakups. I'm counseling every girl on my team through breakups and every girl on other teams through breakups. It's ridiculous.

—*Jeff Griggs*

I felt that when I had cast that company that a lot of the members in that company were much stronger improvisers than I was and I wasn't very self-assured with my directing. But it took a lot of time for me to recognize that I did have value as a director and that my input was valid and that I knew what I was doing...I actually think it wasn't until a year into that ensemble where I felt like I could really hold my own as a director but I think that by that time, it was almost too far gone. It was maybe even more than a year. There was just a lack of respect, I feel, for me as a director because I was never truly confident in myself or it took me too long to become confident in my skills as a director.

—*Kevin Patrick Robbins*

I had to do that thing that I hope I never have to do in a rehearsal process but I did, I said, "Look, this is the situation. Rehearsal starts at three o'clock and you have two options, we either start the rehearsal without you if you're not here and when you get here you have to catch up and explain to everybody why you weren't here. Or if enough people are not here for me to warrant a quality rehearsal, I'm going home and you're on your own." I had to do that I think one time, three people were late out of the nine people cast or whatever and they showed up and I was gone, and they looked around and were like, "Where's Mark?" and the people there were like, "He went home, he wasn't going to wait on you." And then no one was ever late for the rest of the process.

—*Mark Sutton*

A few years ago (mid 90's, I suck at remembering specific dates) I directed a show that had a lot of very talented people in it. It was scenic and musical and the first couple of weeks of rehearsals were great. I started to have problems with one of my players about being on time, and having to miss rehearsals...all that shit. The mood of the cast was going south because there was a degradation in the enthusiasm in the group due to not everyone attending every rehearsal, especially this one very talented guy. He had a bunch of stuff going on that he had to attend to, ran his own company, blah-blah-blah, all kinds of excuses as to why he had to be late/miss rehearsal....so, I made him the star.

I'd played with the idea of a narrator in this form, driving the piece in a Johnstonian kind of way, and decided that I would make him that, so that, "The entire cast, AND SHOW", depended on the unique qualities that he could bring to this show...in the function as narrator. Now, there were others that could have played the narrator that were fine, but this guy was especially great at it, and I suspected that my gamble of giving the most irresponsible person, the greatest responsibility would pay off, and it did.

The cast loved the choice, both for the sense that it made in terms of the talent the guy had, as well as the way I pimped him into having to be there for rehearsal. They'd been in a shitty mood because it was like he was getting special consideration, because his behavior said that he didn't give a shit about the show as much as anyone else. He gave a shit more once he was the key to it's success. I don't give a damn what his motivation was in recommitting to the show, it just worked. The show was great, in part, because of the gamble I made, BUT we couldn't extend the run, because he had other shit going on. He ended up on Main Stage at Second City.

—*Joe Bill*

AFTERWORD AND ACKNOWLEDGEMENTS

Now that I have shown you techniques and philosophies concerning the directing, coaching or teaching of improvisation, it is time for you to make your own decisions. Consider this book a starting point from which to build your own methods and exercises, even your own theories on how to get the best out of your improvisers.

This book contains over a decade of personal experience combined with the wisdom of those who have come before me and run alongside, but it is nothing without your own interpretations. Remember, there are infinite "ways" and eventually, you will find your own. I hope that this book helps make that search easier.

One thing a good director needs to admit is when they don't know something. Even with all the interviews and research there will still be questions left unanswered. I made this book as definitive as I could. Anything else, I don't know, yet.

I wish to thank all the brilliant improvisational directors and teachers who lent their thoughts and experiences to this book to help make it more definitive through interviews, both formal and informal: Armando Diaz, Jill Bernard, Joe Bill, Robert Dassie, Michael Gellman, Jeff Griggs, Don Hall, Tim Kazurinsky, Kevin Mullaney, Mick Napier, Dan O'Connor, Jonathan Pitts, Shira Piven, Michael Pollock, Kevin Patrick Robbins, Jamey Rosen, Gary Schwartz, Rebecca Sohn, Todd Stashwick, and Mark Sutton. Your inclusion was mandatory to me.

An immense amount of gratitude go to Dirty South Improv, a growing company dedicated to the art of improvisation, who helped make the launch of this book possible. It is with great honor that I feature their logo on the back cover. I hope there is more that YESand and DSI can create together in the future.

Don Schuerman, this may be the first you are hearing of this but there was a talk we had about coaching and directing as we were walking through Toronto which was the start of this project for me. Thanks for the bee in my bonnet.

An undying appreciation goes out to all who I taught and who let me teach. This art quickly became my main passion and every chance to explore it further was like a hit of ecstacy. I especially appreciate those who went along with me on my crazy explorations of some new idea, despite being half-baked or possibly off-the-mark, and gave the supportive enthusiasm I needed to make sense of it.

I want to thank all the people I have had the privilege to learn from in classes and rehearsals. I want to particularly thank Len Schiff, my first improv director. Len, if you hadn't done your job so right, I wouldn't still be as excited as I am about improv.

I want to thank all the great improvisers I have had the chance to perform with, which I think is the greatest learning experience. Some of you were slumming by playing with me. I will own up to that, proudly.

Extra thanks to Michael Pollock who pointed me in the right direction in the world of self-publishing (the biggest help being *The Self-Publishing Manual* by Dan Poynter) and Frank Dellario, my business manager who rolled up his shirt sleeves to go through the muck of this venture so I could focus more on writing. These pages would never have been produced without the help of either of them.

Rob Morse, who made the dazzling cover that adorns the book and made it so easy for me to communicate my vision as to what I wanted it to look like. I almost cried the final product was so beautiful.

John Woodley, whose exemplary copyediting and proofreading skills not only refined what text I handed him but forever changed my future writings by showing me how much I hide behind qualifiers and adverbs— most definitely.

I could not have gotten through this book at all if it were not for the insights of my editor, Jill Bernard (whose own *Little Book of Improvisation* is available for sale through the website). Jill, you helped me when I was going crazy both from an overabundance of ideas or a severe lack.

Some others who have helped me throughout the years in varied ways: business partner Karen Herr, marketing guru Stacey Hallal, webmaster extraordinaire Kevin Patrick Robbins, the exceptional illustrator Mike Short, and the business-savvy Zach Ward and Ross White.

My family who, in time, understood that this crazy improv theatre thing was something that I needed to do and gave me all the support I needed. To Mom, Dad, and Merav, I hope this is something that you can show off proudly, and to my niece, Virginia, my favorite person to improvise with.

Most of all, Adrianne, my wife and confidante who sacrificed having time together with me so that I could isolate myself with the task of writing. This included weekends away so I could attend another festival and nights out where I was teaching yet another class, all in the name of developing further fodder for this book. I love you, Adrianne, and now that this beast is done, I want nothing more than to stay under the covers with you.

ABOUT THE AUTHOR

ASAF RONEN is the creator and Editor-in-Chief of YESand.com, a website devoted to improvisation. He has been involved in improv since 1990, starting in college and working with New York Theatresports, NY ComedySportz and directing his own longform improv troupe, Hiatus, where he helped create original longform formats. Asaf has taught improvisation at festivals and through regional theaters, visiting with troupes to hone their skills in Canada, Great Britain, Norway and across these United States. His directing credits include the all-girl group *goga*, the improvised comic book adventure show *Ka-Baam!!*, The Scene, of which he was a founding member, and *Death in the City*, a dramatic longform improv piece at the NY Fringe Festival. Asaf has taught throughout NYC's public schools through LEAP and New Horizons and as part of Weist-Barron's ACTeen program and has freelanced through many theater programs. In 2000, Asaf worked with Cirque du Soleil as a scout for improvisational talent. In his spare time, he likes to breathe.

ABOUT THE EDITOR

JILL BERNARD is the Minneapolis Editor for YESand.com and a regular columnist for Improvland.com. She has been published in the Siren in Minneapolis, MN and was the editor of the Coe College Cosmos in Cedar Rapids, IA. She is the author of *Jill Bernard's Small Cute Book of Improv* and *Short Stories to Delight and Obfuscate*. In addition, Jill has performed with ComedySportz-Twin Cities since 1993, and is the director of their workshop program. She is a founding member of Huge Theater. Her one-woman improv piece, Drum Machine, has been featured at Red Curtain Cabaret, Improv-A-Go-Go, the Chicago Improv Festival, the Toronto Improv Jamboree, Philadelphia's Female Funny Fest, and the ComedySportz National Tournament. She has taught improv all over the country, including Juneau, AK; Spokane, WA; Washington DC; Portland, OR; at the Dirty South Improv Festival, the Funny Woman Fest, and the Tiny Funny Woman Fest. In 2005, she was awarded the Chicago Improv Festival Avery Schreiber Ambassador of Improv Award.